DESIGN
BASICS
MADE EASY

This is a **FLAME TREE** book
First published 2016

Publisher and Creative Director: Nick Wells
Project Editor: Polly Prior
Picture Research: Catherine Taylor and Josie Mitchell
Art Director and Layout Design: Mike Spender
Digital Design and Production: Chris Herbert

FLAME TREE PUBLISHING
6 Melbray Mews
Fulham, London SW6 3NS
United Kingdom

www.flametreepublishing.com

16 18 20 19 17
1 3 5 7 9 10 8 6 4 2

A CIP record for this book is available from the British Library upon request.

ISBN: 978-1-78361-595-7

Printed in China | Created, Developed & Produced in the United Kingdom

Images courtesy of Shutterstock and © the following photographers: wavebreakmedia 1, 7(b), 132(b), 135, 197(b), 200(b), 226; Stepan Bormotov 3, 162, 251; rangizzz 4(t), 14; baranq 4(b), 52; scyther5 5(t), 22, 76; donatas1205 5(b), 106; Semisatch 6(t), 136; gabczi 6(b), 160; LuckyDesigner 7(t), 194; Rawpixel.com 8, 10(b), 17(b), 78, 94(b), 247(b); Dmitry Nikolaev 9; Ajgul 10(t); Kekyalyaynen 11; Invisible Studio 12; Mascha Tace 16; Petr Vaclavek 17(t); Kostenko Maxim 29; Deamles for Sale 47; M.Photos 55; mrs.kato 58; Olga Miltsova 61(l); Chunni4691 65; Shchipkova Elena 80; Pressmaster 86; Repina Valeriya 88(b); Luciano Mortula 89(b, r); Jane Rix 100; everything possible 104(t); create jobs 51 141; Stuart Miles 146(b); Mumemories 163(t); alterfalter 163(b); rzoze19 165(t); everything possible 171(b); Jesus Cervantes 181; Maksym Dykha 184(b); robert_s 187(t, l); Vladyslav Starozhylov 188(b); TungCheung 189(b); Kaspars Grinvalds 196; PinkBlue 197(t); urfin 202(t, l); lumen-digital 204(b); Aaron Amat 206(t); GaudiLab 208; Monkey Business Images 211; FabrikaSimf 212(b); Stokkete 214(t); Marine's 233; My_inspiration 236(t); Raywoo 242(b). Courtesy of Getty Images and © Patrick Demarchelier 139(t, r). Courtesy of Stocksnap and © the following: Milada Vigerova 22; Luis Llerena 28; Chalffy Chan 29; Annie Spratt 33; Martin Miranda/Maxwell Davis/Ase Bjøntegard Oftedal/Ryan McGuire 34, 103; Piotr Lohunko 37; Jay Mantri 44; Fargana Ismailova 48; Todd Quackenbush 49; Blair Fraser 61(r); Alex Wong 62; Claudiu Sergiu Danaila 64; Jay Wennington 67; Bench Accounting 69; Antoine Beauvillain 71; Joao Silas 72; Jaroslaw Puszczynski 73, 104(b); Eric Haidara 74; Pawel Kadysz 75; kazu end 81(l); Felipe Dolce 81(t); Leeroy 82(t, l); Bench Accounting 82(b); Gili Benita 83(b); Patryk Dziejma 87(b, r); Andreas Rønningen 90(b, r); Skitter Photo 91(t); Danielle MacInnes 91(b); Alexandra Diaconu 92(t); Zoe Magee 92(b); Marcin Milewski 96(b). © Gunter Rambow 139(t, l),139(b). © Immediate Media Company Ltd, 2016 157; © The Liberation SARL 158; © 2015 Adobe Systems Incorporated. All rights reserved. 198, 199(t and b), 200(t), 215(b), 217(b); © Inkscape/Ryan Lerch/CC0 1.0 Universal 201(t, l); © Bohemian Coding 201(t, r); © Blender Foundation, www.blender.org 201(b, r); © Marvel Prototyping Ltd 202(t, r); © InVision 2015 202(b, l); © 2010–2015 UXPin Sp. z o.o 202(b, r); Copyright © 2015 Apple Inc. All rights reserved. 205, 213(t). All other images courtesy of the authors.

DESIGN
BASICS
MADE EASY

AARON MILLER | ANDREA PENNOYER

DAVID WOODWARD | AMBAR GALAN

FLAME TREE
PUBLISHING

CONTENTS

It's sometimes difficult to know where to start with a design, especially if you are a novice or have never designed anything before. This chapter will introduce you to the real basics of digital and graphic design, including the concepts of proximity, balance, contrast and repetition among others. You will gain an understanding of the building blocks of design and their importance in creating impactful work.

The spacing on the page can truly make or break a design; for example, it can mean the difference between an effective, impactful design and one that leaves a key message lost in clutter. This chapter will cover how to achieve harmony and balance in your designs, and what these terms mean in a practical context. It also covers the effective use of white space to bring focus to a piece.

THE RIGHT COLOUR

Working with colour as a designer is a lot more complicated than what colours complement each other. This chapter goes into detail regarding colour combinations that work well in print and on screen, as well as exploring the colour wheel and monochromatic, analogous, complementary and triadic colour schemes.

EFFECTIVE TYPOGRAPHY

A part of creating any good design is finding the right fonts, and using them so that they will have the most impact. Size, leading, tracking and kerning will all change the way your overall design will be viewed and this chapter explains these terms and how to use typography to your advantage. This chapter also covers how to choose a font for different purposes and the importance of hierarchy and scale in creating coherence in your designs.

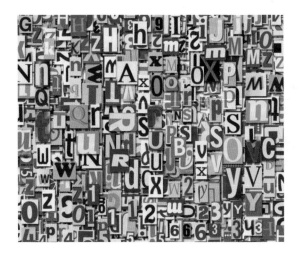

USING IMAGES 136

This chapter brings images to the forefront and explores how to maximize their effect on your design, including how to choose images, where to place them and how they can be combined with text to create a powerful message. Practical advice on copyright issues and converting files will help you to put these skills into practice. Also covered here are tips on manipulating images in Photoshop, to really optimize designs.

DESIGNING FOR PRINT 160

When designing for print there are some rules that it is important to follow to produce a successful design, whether you are designing a book, a flyer, a poster or anything that will be printed. This chapter covers everything you will need to know, including the best software for your project and their advantages and disadvantages; the layout of your document, explaining how to set up the size and where the gutter will be; as well as the importance of colour and resolution; and finally, how to export your project.

DESIGNING FOR SCREEN

Whether you are designing a blog, a professional webpage or even an advert, this chapter will introduce you to everything that it is important to consider to create fantastic designs for screens. Usability and the impact of the layout are both explored, as well as the differences between designing for a desktop screen and a smartphone. This chapter delves into the best fonts to use on the web, resolution and the basics of coding and how your webpage will work.

WORKING WITH OTHERS

Whether you've been a professional designer for years, or are just starting out, this overview of taking on a professional project can provide you with helpful tips and tricks. Covering the process from taking on a brief, undertaking the design, right through to delivering the final file, there is nothing left out.

FURTHER READING & USEFUL WEBSITES

INDEX

INTRODUCTION

Graphic design is, in simple terms, the art and practice of communicating an experience or idea, combining text and graphics to convey an effective message. The form can be physical, such as print, or digital, such as a website.

DESIGN IS EVERYWHERE

Graphic design is the most universal of all the arts. It is all around us. We are bombarded with advertisements, logos, colours and shapes, whether at the supermarket, walking down the high street or watching TV. We often take this for granted, forgetting each advert has been carefully

considered and executed by a designer or design team. It can also be surprising to think of the number of people involved in the creative process: a copywriter, planner, designer, art director, pre-press manager and creative director.

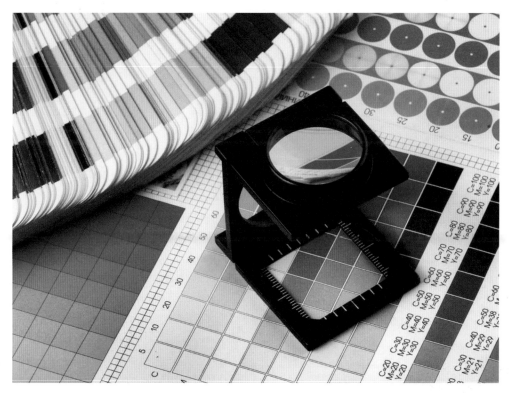

Above: Learn how to apply colour theory, get the most out of the software and take your designs to the next level.

Design in Action!

For hundreds of years, designers have arranged type and images on posters, advertisements, packaging and other printed media – and now, increasingly on the internet – to help catch our eye and hold our attention. Clever graphic design engages with us, inviting us to think about a product or service in a certain light, without us even realizing it.

Iconography

Design doesn't always need words to be understood; think about, for example, the stick figures used for male and female toilet signs. These work in any language, anywhere in the world and have a universally recognized meaning. This symbolic representation of a subject, or iconography, is a quick, visual method for communicating information, serving designers every day, helping them solve design challenges.

Right: Icons can really help designers to communicate across languages, and very quickly. The light bulb icon, for example, stands for a new idea.

DESIGN BASICS MADE EASY

You don't have to have a degree to become a graphic designer. A creative mind, an eye for detail and this book under one arm are all you need to learn and improve. Whether you're just starting out as a designer, wanting to keep up to date with design trends or brushing up on your technical knowledge, *Design Basics Made Easy* is the perfect resource. By using this book, you will learn tricks and tips from practising graphic and digital designers that will improve your design skill-set.

Left: Using this book, you will learn all about designing for screen.

Little by Little

Graphic design is a broad subject. This book could easily be five times as long, spanning thousands of pages, but we've whittled it down into short, digestible, clearly defined chapters. At times the subject matter will overlap and touch briefly on something that has its own dedicated chapter; if this is the case, we will point you in the right direction to find out more.

Quick Tips!

Throughout this book, we have included a number of Quick Tips. These are designed to help you find simple yet effective methods and techniques which will help you become a better designer. Shortcuts and insightful ways of working will speed up your productivity, meaning there is more time available to spend on creative work: perfect!

Easily Digestible

Make no mistake, there's a lot of information contained within the next 250 pages or so, but there's no need to be intimidated. In some areas we offer a general explanation of design principles or theory; in others there are detailed, step-by-step instructions. We have also

illustrated every chapter with multiple screenshots to help enhance what is being explained in the text. This book is not designed to be read cover to cover in one sitting. Think of it more as a how-to guide, one that you can pick up and put down, as and when you need it.

Jargon Busting

It is true that some jargon is unavoidable, but wherever possible we've attempted to explain and break down technical terms in easy-to-understand language.

EIGHT CHAPTERS

Design Basics Made Easy has eight expertly written chapters by design professionals, including typographers, illustrators and print masters.

Chapter One is all about the importance of the building blocks of graphic design: the principles. These include proximity, alignment, repetition, contrast and balance. Chapter Two gets you thinking about the importance of spatial awareness within your designs: how to utilize white space and bring harmony and balance to the page. In Chapter Three you will discover the power of colour and in Chapter Four we jump in at the deep end with one of the most important, yet often overlooked, elements of design: typography. In Chapter Five you will learn about imagery, whether you are editing images or combining them with type.

Left: Apply some typographic rules to your design, including readability, legibility and balance.

Chapter Six is all about designing for print: tackling margins, gutters and page bleed, as well as understanding the limitations of print, exporting files and communicating with a printer. In Chapter Seven we run through designing for screen, explaining current trends, new ways of working, resolution restrictions and looking at what is next for responsive web design. Finally, Chapter Eight discusses collaboration with others on a project, from taking an initial brief, understanding the tech specifications, handling criticism and feedback, how to deliver your final design and, finally, how to handle deadlines!

APPS & SOFTWARE

The number of software packages available for designers can seem a little overwhelming at first. To help you out, we have picked the most widely used software so that you can choose a package to meet your needs, whether you are working on a print project, designing a logo or colour-correcting a batch of photographs. The most commonly used industry software comes with a hefty price tag, but we have provided some great free alternatives, perfect for those new to design.

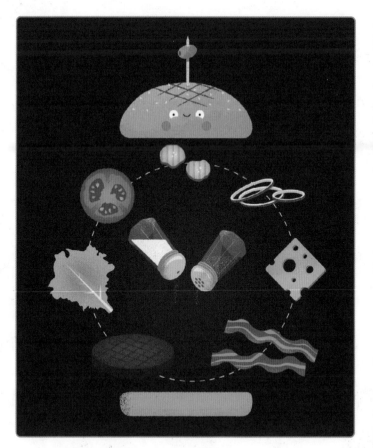

Right: An example of Aaron Miller's illustration work. Here you see a self-initiated project based around burgers!

GETTING THE BASICS RIGHT

THE BUILDING BLOCKS OF DESIGN

Graphic design's buildings blocks include proximity, alignment, repetition, contrast and balance. They are applied to design elements (line, shape, text/typography, image, scale, colour) and help designers achieve visually pleasing and strategically effective designs for their clients.

COMMUNICATION IS KEY

A designer's job is always one of function. Creative expression is an important part of design, but graphic design must always solve a communication problem too. 'What must your design achieve?' is a question to ask repeatedly.

Using Building Blocks to Good Effect

The best designs in the world, the designs we are most drawn to, most affected by, look as though they were composed effortlessly. They look as though their elements were casually and quickly arranged to achieve a unified, beautiful

Right: Communicating the information you need to should always be one of your highest priorities.

and compelling 'voice'. But the truth is that the best designs have undergone countless iterations – or versions – fine-tuning details to an exactitude that seems unreasonable.

A book cover, for example, may have had up to (and possibly more than) 50 iterations, all exploring different concepts, visual arrangements, typefaces, colours and sizes, each achieving a slightly different result. The final design represents hundreds of hours of experimenting with fundamentals, such as proximity, alignment, repetition, contrast and balance.

Above: The final design for a book cover can take many, many revisions and versions before it is perfected. Sometimes the best way to get started is to use a template.

A Sum of its Parts

This chapter looks at these fundamentals (proximity, alignment, repetition, contrast and balance), and shows you how, when they are used well, a designer can present a unified and effective design – a whole that is visually the sum of its parts.

THE BUILDING BLOCKS

Graphic design's buildings blocks (e.g. proximity, alignment, repetition) are applied to design elements (e.g. line, shape, text/typography, image, scale and colour) and help designers achieve visually pleasing and strategically effective designs for their clients.

SOLVING CHALLENGES

Building blocks can also help solve graphic design challenges. Perhaps you are designing a banner ad for a client who has asked you to include what feels like too much content for such a limited size. Playing with the proximity of elements, for example, may be the starting point for sorting through what feels like an impossible feat.

Quick Tip

The building blocks of design need not be limited to your professional practice. Exploring them in painting, photography, collage or crafting not only makes you more comfortable working with them, but can also yield surprising visual results, which you can later use for a client.

PEAK TO PEAK MMXVI

August 8th, **RISE TO THE CHALLENGE**. Starting near treeline, you climb over 2000 feet to the summit of Babcock Mountain. There you claim your reward in the spectacular open terrain at the top of the mountain as you begin the descent home.

You want a half marathon you can *really* talk about? **CLICK HERE** and **RISE TO THE CHALLENGE!** WWW.P2P.COM

PEAK TO PEAK MMXVI
You want a half marathon you can *really* talk about?
CLICK HERE and **RISE TO THE CHALLENGE!**

August 8th, **RISE TO THE CHALLENGE**. Starting at treeline, climb over 2000 feet to the summit of Babcock Mountain. There you claim your reward in the spectacular open terrain at the top of the mountain as you begin the descent home.

WWW.P2P.COM

Above: The top banner shows raw materials separated according to client's file. The bottom banner uses overlapping, which provides the space to enlarge the text and connect the event with the location in a more dynamic way.

PROXIMITY

Generally speaking, people use 'proximity' to refer to nearness, which can apply to space, time and occurrence. But in graphic design, proximity refers to how close elements are to each other spatially, and what that relationship achieves.

CONSIDERING PROXIMITY

Thinking through proximity carefully in your graphic design can achieve several things, including sophistication and hierarchy. These and many more are explored in the following pages.

Above: The strongest relationships are rarely simple line-by-line arrangements but groupings of elements arranged to be readable – to serve the design's messaging purpose – and to be visually balanced.

Left: Simply changing fonts, colour and sizes does not achieve a desired result. **Middle:** Interpreting more directly with the text results in more visual interest and a more legible hierarchy. **Right:** Flier with raw text as received from a client.

Sophistication

When a graphic designer accepts a project, they are usually provided with some plain text, indicating the basic message required by the client. Some simple font and colour changes, something an amateur may do, will not suffice as a complete project. You have been hired for your ability to visually interpret raw material, and creating spatial relationships between elements proves that you are thinking beyond the obvious and drawing meaning out of the client's message. Graphic designers do not just make things pretty. They speak visually.

Hierarchy

To establish a visual hierarchy is to determine what pieces of information are most important, and which are least important (and points in between). Proximity can help with this. A large, solitary image or word occupying much of your artboard could easily be recognized as the most important. Smaller elements positioned further away could be secondary and tertiary.

Quick Tip

Related to hierarchy is emphasis. Grouping elements together in a particular proximity to each other can guide your audience through the information hierarchy, but doing so without applying other building blocks – contrast, for example – keeps a good design from being a great one.

TURRIS FORTIS DEUS NOSTER

INSPIRING HEARTS & MINDS

Above: This minimal cover design for a university brochure utilises the school's heraldry rather than a conventional title to intentionally draw attention to its heritage.

Dynamics

There is an energy that two or more objects positioned close to each other can generate. When graphic elements are placed in close proximity, an added layer of meaning may result. The audience immediately 'reads' a connection between the word ('Sale') and the image underneath, and instantaneously appreciates the relationship between the sales event and the product available. Think through your messaging and remember that where the type sits in relationship to other graphic components can clarify or confuse a message.

Below: Keep in mind that the position of text is very important. Here the word 'Sale' is linked with clothing in the design on the right, making it more effective than the other design.

Tension

Sometimes, overlapping elements can unintentionally change negative space into a shape that then becomes a visual distraction. Train your eye to see the negative spaces, and your mind to think of them not as unused real estate but elements in themselves. Visually, they are as active as the positives, the elements on your artboard (see page 54).

Left: The negative spaces in the design at the top are taken into consideration, leading to a clearer message.

A ROUNDTABLE REVIEW

MONEY & THE MEANING OF LIFE
By Jacob Needleman
—
Peter Mogan

NCE IN A WHILE, a book comes along that changes your life. I don't mean that it gives you a new way of looking at things, or a new insight, or even concrete steps for making a life change—I am talking about actual, implemented, lasting change. *Money and the Meaning of Life* by Jacob Needleman was such a book for me. Let me explain.

It was ten years ago, my friend, Patty, was about to embark on a new venture leading workshops on "money messages" and asked if I would be a "guinea pig" in her first group. I happily agreed. She told me that the woman who had developed this workshop was a very successful financial advisor who had come to the realization that all of her clients held, to some extent, powerful, subconscious money messages that impacted their relationship with money in a negative way. This insight led her to read Needleman's book and develop the workshop.

After reading the book and taking the workshop, I realized that I have lived all of my adult life with the deeply held conviction—albeit subconscious—that financial disaster is just around the corner. It made sense that I had formed this conviction because I came from a family that had experienced bankruptcy three times. As my professional practice grew and became more financially stable, an ugly twist was added. As a result, I was living with fear and was desperately trying to ward off the inevitable collapse. This fear affected how I thought, what I felt, how I acted, and even how I related to my family. But because it was all under the surface, I was living in its power without any real awareness. When I was able to articulate my false money message to the group at the workshop, I

Breathing Room

Graphics in close proximity are effective. But perhaps it is most appropriate to keep elements far away from each other in order to keep messaging clear and uninterrupted. Giving certain elements breathing space may keep text readable or ensure that the perfectly selected photograph you searched high and low for is given its space to shine. White space is a powerful tool in graphic design and will be addressed in the next chapter (see page 71).

Right: This title page for a book review has opted for its title and body text to be separated by white space to maintain the minimal theme of the rest of the publication. The blue dropcap "O" connects the title and the text.

ALIGNMENT

Like proximity, alignment is not exclusive to graphic design – it is something we recognize daily. But it does have a specific role in graphic design. By visually connecting elements together, your layouts can be ordered and your message clearly communicated. And like much in graphic design, working with alignment requires both a calculated and intuitive approach.

WHAT DOES ALIGNMENT LOOK LIKE?

The building blocks of design are invisible. We do not see proximity. We do not see alignment. As mentioned earlier, they are principles. What we see are the results of building blocks having been applied. Think about your word processing software. Our text is routinely aligned left, centre or

Above: Alignment is a core building block that will impact the whole design.

Right: We would not be able to read text easily without alignment.

shall be late!' (when she thought it over afterwards, it ought to have wondered at this, but at the time it all when the Rabbit actually took a watch out of its wai at it, and then hurried on, Alice started to her feet, fo that she had never before seen a rabbit with either a v to take out of it, and burning with curiosity, she ran fortunately was just in time to see it pop down a larg hedge.

In another moment down went Alice after it, ne in the world she was to get out again.

The rabbit-hole went straight on like a tunnel fo dipped suddenly down, so suddenly that Alice had n stopping herself before she found herself falling dow the well was very deep, or she fell very slowly, for sh went down to look about her and to wonder what w First, she tried to look down and make out what she too dark to see anything; then she looked at the sides that they were filled with cupboards and book-shelve maps and pictures hung upon pegs. She took down a as she passed; it was labelled 'ORANGE MARMALADE', b ment it was empty: she did not like to drop the jar fo so managed to put it into one of the cupboards as she right. We do not actually see the lines the text is running along but we know they are there. Especially as the text gets longer – the longer the text, the more evident the margin is. The text's edge goes from suggesting an invisible line to actually creating one.

ALIGNMENT AND GRID SYSTEMS

Grids will be properly introduced in the next chapter (see page 56), but it's worth mentioning them now. A grid system provides a structure for establishing where graphic elements are positioned on a page. They comprise vertical and horizontal lines, along which elements can be aligned and connected. Because we find certain structures more visually comfortable, grids help us design arrangements that are readable and aesthetically attractive.

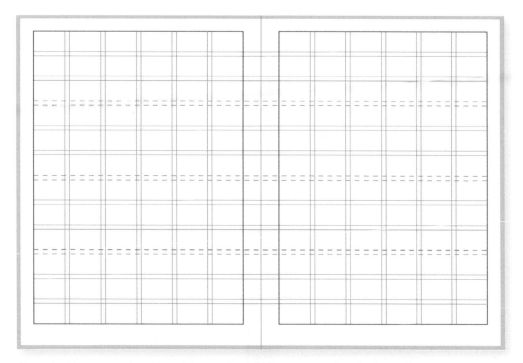

Above: A grid structure such as this one is immensely helpful for creating aesthetically pleasing designs.

WHAT CAN ALIGNMENT ACHIEVE?

When graphic elements are aligned, their edges create imaginary lines extending from the edges of shapes, text margins, subjects in photographs, and so on. These lines can help establish an order for your graphic elements.

Hierarchy

Our eyes are inclined to follow a visual path. Well-aligned elements can 'point' us first to the most important piece of information (a title, for example) and direct us next to a secondary point, which can lead us to a third, and so on. This does not mean that stacking the information in order of importance from top to bottom is a solution. We have a more sophisticated way of viewing design. It means that, combined with proximity, contrast, balance, colour

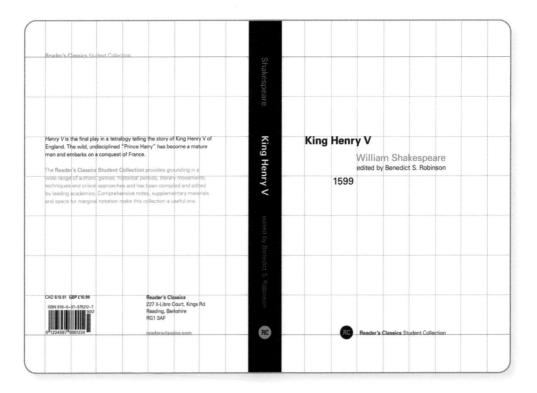

(see 'The Right Colour', page 76) and so on, alignment aids in emphasizing what is most important, regardless of where it is located on your artboard.

Quick Tip

Always reassess the decisions you make in the best interest of aesthetics (how attractive, how beautiful it is) on the basis of your communication needs. Ask yourself whether how you have arranged the elements helps or hinders the mandate of your project and your client.

Left & Below: The front and back cover of a book using alignment of text to establish hierarchy. Note how the grid aids the placement of the words to create a visual path.

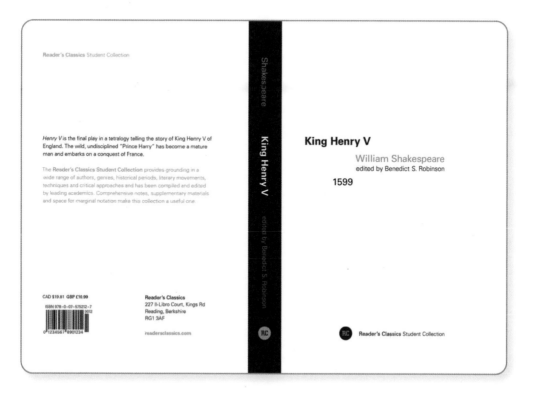

Structure

You would not drive across a bridge without railings. Even though you technically could do so, it would be anxiety-inducing. The same (albeit less dangerous) principle applies here. Humans like to sense boundaries. Using lines to arrange graphics builds order. It keeps a design from seeming chaotic by providing paths and boundaries for the viewer.

SHANICE S. FENTON   ILLUSTRATION & ART

shanicesfenton.com
hello@shanicesfenton.com

604 555 5052

Above: Standard structures help us to interpret information easily and quickly.

Sophistication

Alignment can elevate your design professionally, by indicating a working knowledge of graphic design principles. Using the building blocks together brings sophistication to your designs, and can bring about a more suitable and exciting end product.

Quick Tip

A familiar alignment fall-back is simply to centre your text and images, giving little consideration to the message and its target audience. By feeding yourself a diet of quality graphic design examples to keep abreast of both trends and timeless fundamentals, you will dodge amateur foibles.

Mary Lamb

the EMINENT WOMEN SERIES

by MRS. GILCHRIST   *Ed.* JOHN H. INGRAM

Preface

I am indebted to Mrs. Henry Watson, a granddaughter of Mr. Gillman, for one or two interesting reminiscences, and for a hitherto unpublished "notelet" by Lamb (p. 248), together with an omitted paragraph from a published letter (p. 84), which confirms what other letters also show.---that the

Left: This example shows a title and its subheadings aligned along a centre axis, but divides them to help move the eye across the page horizontally. The subsequent paragraph is aligned left.

ALIGNMENT TIPS

How do you actually apply alignment to your design? Here are some simple tips to get you started.

Seeing Lines

The first step is seeing lines and edges in your graphic elements – all the elements. Do not limit yourself to text and shape. Photography and illustration also have lines. Yes, they exist around their frames, but they are also present in their subjects. These built-in guides provide us with a starting place from which to align other graphics.

Right: It is important to see lines even in photography and illustrations. Here, your eye is naturally drawn up to the text from the centre line of the photograph.

Do not dwell in the past, do not dream of the future, concentrate the mind on the present moment.
BUDDHA

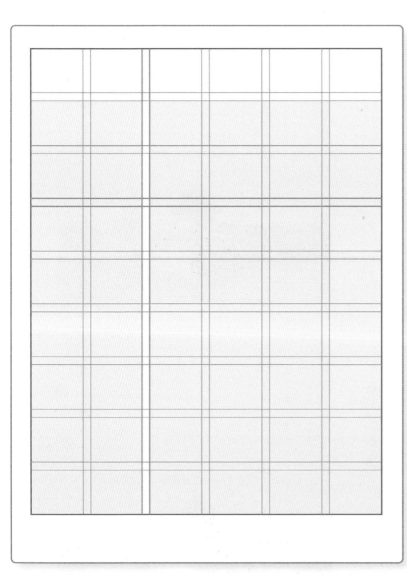

Above: Here is an example of a grid with margins (in orange) and columns and rows (in blue). There are major divisions after column two and row three indicating where primary material can be placed.

Making a Grid

Again, this will be expanded upon in our next chapter (see page 56), but dividing your artboard into evenly spaced rows and columns is the very first thing to do with your file. It will certainly direct you from then on.

Margins

Your grid's margins provide a simple and straightforward start for aligning objects. While having images bleed off the end of a design is certainly a way to make your design dynamic, your central information must be comfortable to read. Margins provide a container, keeping important information from getting too close to that other invisible line: the artboard's edge.

Arrangements to Try

Here are six basic alignment arrangements to get you started. It might seem like common sense to align elements to the left or the right, but it may surprise you how often the simplest solutions can be overlooked. Try these and discern how your message is affected as you experiment.

Below: Experimenting with different arrangements such as these can help you to find a better design.

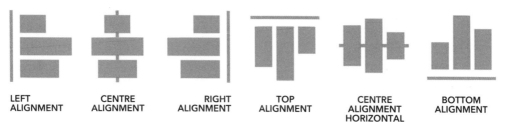

LEFT
ALIGNMENT

CENTRE
ALIGNMENT

RIGHT
ALIGNMENT

TOP
ALIGNMENT

CENTRE
ALIGNMENT
HORIZONTAL

BOTTOM
ALIGNMENT

Play Around with Alignment

Aligning elements requires some experimentation (as do all the building blocks). Alignment is one tool that works to ensure layouts are visually satisfying and ordered, two things a viewer needs.

FLIP & NOT FLOP
by JASON CHAN

Are we naturally good? Are we predisposed to act cooperatively and help others even when it costs us? Or are we selfish creatures?

Evolutionary theorists have traditionally focused on competition and the ruthlessness of natural selection, but often they have failed to consider a critical fact: that humans could not have survived in nature without the charity and social reciprocity of a group through the

Quick Tip

Try using more than one of the above alignment arrangements in a composition. Mixing a centred alignment with an asymmetrical one (see 'Balance' on page 45, and in the next chapter) is tricky, so it's best to start with aligning elements along the left and then the right. Doing so can accomplish a sense of movement, of energy.

Left: Mixing alignments up in the same design can give energy to your work, but it must not be overdone or it will distract and confuse.

REPETITION

Repetition is clarifying. It is hard to avoid. Think of the many ways repetition is used outside of graphic design. So much of how we engage with our world is based on familiar patterns, messages, cues and sounds. A warning light at a level crossing has more impact when it is blinking than when it is lit solid. We know, by virtue of the repetition, that we need to pay attention.

WHAT REPETITION IS NOT

Before progressing, it is necessary to state that repetition is not pattern. Pattern is a sequence of repeated elements that are the same. Repetition uses elements that are varied. The variation keeps us engaged, keeps us interested, keeps us from assuming that we have gleaned all there is from it.

Right: Repetition can be used to draw attention to design elements that are varied.

Quick Tip

Graphic designers specializing in textiles or surface graphics use pattern to make texture. Keep an eye out for graphics printed on clothing or backpacks, and note how they differ in purpose from a website or poster campaign.

WHAT REPETITION ACHIEVES

Repetition does not mean literally copying and pasting the same image in several locations. It means recognizing a visual quality and using it repeatedly to emphasize a point, establish a style, and help people know how to navigate through various design elements (a campaign or a multipage document or website).

Above: On the left is a repeated pattern and on the right is an example of repetition. They are quite different.

Left: A suite of material repeatedly using similar graphic elements achieves a unified visual voice while keeping different communication pieces distinct.

Emphasis

Repeating elements not only makes a point, but it makes the point clearer. It emphasizes. When we see an element recurrently, an audience is being told the same message over and over, thereby emphasizing its importance. In graphic design, this could be a subtle effect (the repetition of a colour scheme, for example) or the overt restating of a single word to drive a point home.

Above: The repetition of shape unifies the webpage and emphasizes the featured content: people.

Unity of Style

Elements that share graphic characteristics can give your design a particular style. Using the same colour combinations, imagery, line weights, typefaces, light source (photography), illustration style and so on, establishes a visual theme, unifying your design.

Below: Giving your design a specific style and repeating this throughout will bring all of the elements together to create a unified, powerful impression.

Quick Tip

One place to glean inspiration for repetition is in the cover design for a series of books. There is power in numbers, and the visual strength that a shared graphic theme performs in a bookstore makes them hard to miss.

Right: Repeating a design style on the spines of books makes them stand out on a bookshelf.

Visual Consistency

Think about how repetition applies to multipage documents or campaigns consisting of multiple pieces. To repeat the same element throughout a communications strategy provides visual stability and marketing strength, and aids in navigating multiple pages. Your audience will know that it is viewing the same public awareness campaign over the course of several months or that it is still reading the same section in an online magazine.

Quick Tip

In projects with multiple modes of communication, think beyond the basic layout and make sure every photograph (or illustration) is produced by the same artist. The repetition of style provides another level of consistency essential to a campaign or brand.

In the next chapter (see page 52), you will read more on how grids and repeated elements make navigation of multipage projects (for both print and screen) possible.

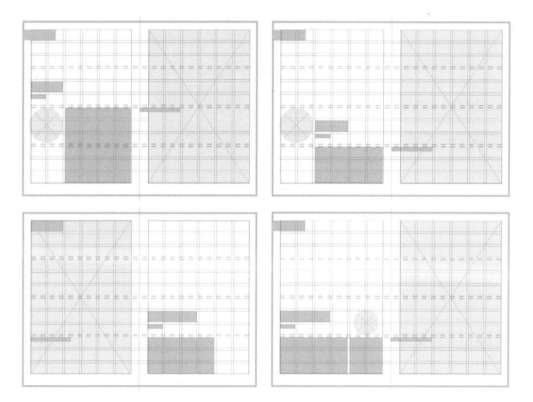

Above: Grids are invaluable, especially when creating multipage projects.

REPETITION AND MONOTONY

Be careful – too much of the same thing can be very boring. It is not only dull, it can affect a design in the very opposite way you intend. Without variation and without a solid idea of what your design needs to achieve, repeated elements cease to engage an audience and take on another role entirely, that of pattern. So how does a graphic designer avoid sameness?

Variation

Think of a zebra's stripes. They are all the same, right? Yes. And no. They have the same features: long, wavy and black. But the intervals of waves differ from stripe to stripe. This is variation. Basic qualities carry the graphic theme, but slight difference keeps a composition interesting and functional.

Above: The difference in a zebra's stripes is a perfect example from nature of how variation in repetition makes an impact.

Quick Tip

Nature is consistently one of the best ways to recognize visual patterns, shapes, colour and contrast. Visually, it is naturally unified and provides endless points of inspiration, which can be applied to your work.

Content

If your design's content (its message) is inherently connected to repetition as a way of emphasis, your design will avoid monotony. Ask yourself, what does my message need to emphasize? Using repetition to reinforce a message gives your design purpose and keeps it appealing.

ALL IN FOR CHARITY

TEXAS HOLD 'EM TOURNAMENT
100% of proceeds go to the Stronger Together Foundation

Above: Repetition is a fantastic way to enhance your key message.

CONTRAST

Think juxtaposition. Think light and dark, up and down, small and large, thin and thick, near and far, straight and round, shiny and matte.

WHAT CONTRAST ACHIEVES

As you have probably noticed, our building blocks of design overlap in their purposes and in their effects. There can be contrast in how elements are grouped in proximity to each other. There can be contrast in the variation of repeated elements. There is often contrast in colour schemes (see the chapter on 'The Right Colour', page 76).

Below: The differences in the sizes and the smooth and sharp edges of these shapes make the design memorable.

And you can achieve effective contrast in the typefaces you select for text (see the 'Effective Typography' chapter, page 106). Enhancing the differences of elements can make your design visually dynamic and functionally successful. Using contrast can achieve a number of effects.

Emphasis

It can often seem as though every building block we have discussed achieves emphasis, but emphasis is contrast's inherent role. When two different objects are juxtaposed, a relationship

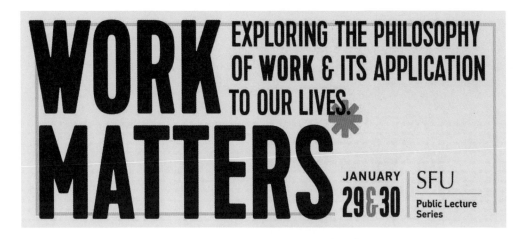

Above: Emphasizing important words in your design can create a strong message.

is formed that forces an emphasis – either a visual emphasis and/or a messaging emphasis.

Modest Exaggeration

By having two elements in contrast, you are exaggerating their inherent qualities. A red Christmas ornament looks strikingly red when hanging on a green tree. A newspaper's main headline seems much bigger when followed by 8 pt text.

Right: This menu design contrasts an ornate, antique etching against a heavy, contemporary typeface.

TO DO IT
Throwing Caution to
the Wind

BY
Samantha Grant

Contrast and Concept

A fitness guru eating dinner at McDonald's. A businessman skateboarding to a meeting. Two graphics with independent associations can mean something completely different when combined. They can be posed in the same photograph or placed in close proximity to each other. Top advertising agencies know that meaning derived from contrast cannot be overlooked.

Left: This book cover concept is working with the client's interest in connecting performance with a leap of faith.

Quick Tip

Go to the fiction section in your local bookshop. Notice how contrast is used to convey complicated and abstract concepts. The saying goes, 'Don't judge a book by its cover,' but a good designer assumes that customers are doing just that.

MAKING CONTRAST

Now that we know that contrast goes beyond offsetting a circle with a square (though this is a good technique), what can you do to increase contrast in your project?

Above: Contrasting colours can make or break a design.

Contrasting Colour

The chapter on 'The Right Colour' (see page 76) will delve into colour schemes in depth, but suffice to say that colour is a very effective and powerful way to achieve instant contrast. The colour wheel will guide you in your swatch selection to ensure that your contrasting colours are still unified.

Quick Tip

Do not have too much fun mixing and matching fonts. You will only need a maximum of three typefaces for any one project. Too many will compromise your design's overall unity of voice.

Contrast from White Space

What could be more differentiating than the contrast between something (a graphic element) and nothing (a design's artboard)? We will explore white space in more detail in the next chapter (see page 52).

Contrasting Typography

Typefaces can add visual interest and help distinguish a title from a subtitle, a heading from the main text. You want to pair typefaces that are different (a sans serif font and a serif font) but share a visual voice. See the chapter on 'Effective Typography', page 106.

> # Dame Kiri Te Kanawa opera masterclass
>
> **26 JUNE 2015**
>
> *As part of the BBC Cardiff Singer of the World season, int opera star Dame Kiri Te Kanawa leads a masterclass for fo*
>
> **DAME KIRI WORKS WITH SINGERS,** Celine Forrest, Blaise Malaba, Regula grim and offers a critique on both voice and performance in the Dora Stoutz College of Music and Drama. Accompaniment is provided by pianist Simon

Above: It's important to use different typefaces to distinguish between titles and the main text.

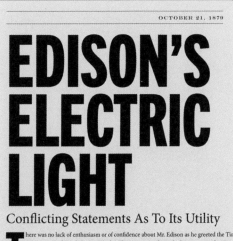

OCTOBER 21, 1879

EDISON'S ELECTRIC LIGHT

Conflicting Statements As To Its Utility

There was no lack of enthusiasm or of confidence about Mr. Edison as he greeted the Tim
oratory at Menlo Park, N. J., yesterday. The inventor, a short, thick-set man, with grimy
workshop, and willingly explained the distinctive features of what he and many others l
will soon cause gas-light to be a thing of the past. The lamp which Mr. Edison regards a
simplicity and economy. In the lamp the light is emitted by a horseshoe of carbonized paper abo
the width of a thread. This horseshoe is in a glass globe, from which the air has been as thoroug
do. So good a vacuum is produced that it is estimated that at the utmost no more than a one-mi
operation of pumping lasts one hour and a quarter. At the ends of the carbon horseshoe are two

Above: Different sizes of text are the most common form of emphasis.

SUBTLE CONTRAST

Thus far in this exploration, we have been referring to obvious, strong contrast, but there are more subtle ways to employ it. This may be very valuable for a project that does not need to be particularly 'loud'. The irony, of course, is that by way of minimal and subtle contrast, your design could stand out more prominently against the less restrained graphic design we encounter day to day.

Contrasting Scale

Using size is an excellent way to emphasize difference. Perhaps a more familiar method than colour, scale not only makes a layout dynamic, but it also helps establish information hierarchy, and can be used to strengthen a metaphor or concept.

UNSP

an inheritance of words · by CONNIE T. BRAUN

OKEN

Fern Hill Publications
SPECIAL EDITION

Above: This book cover uses space and size to contrast the title with the secondary and tertiary lines of text.

Contrast and Story

A metaphor to help us understand how contrast can more subtly strengthen a design is that of a story. From first glance to a final call to action ('Donate now,' 'RSVP,' 'Click here') our eyes follow a trail of graphic emphasis. Although this can occupy all of seconds, we view graphic design in much the same way as we read a narrative arch, requiring a punctuated start, a detailed and supportive middle, and an effective conclusion that motivates us to respond thoughtfully — it is a unified message made up of different pieces that keep the reader progressing. Visual contrast subtly makes distinctions between the connected, unified graphics, and provides a line of emphasis that ends with motivating an audience to respond.

Quick Tip

Using black and white is a good place to start when thinking about how to achieve subtle contrast. The combination of these two 'colours' is most obviously one of contrast. By using thinner typefaces, black and white photos, and ample white space, you could produce a very modern and chic design.

The Impossible Dre

Colonizing Mars

by JANET FISHER, *National Geographic*

The Red Planet has come to symbolize something m
space exploration. Perhaps that explains why, throug
people have granted Mars a *unique spot* in our consci

Above: A good example of how designers create a visual narrative from main title through main text.

Minimalism

The gentle but heavy undulating lines of calligraphy on a cream sheet of paper, a grainy black and white photo, or the minimally applied splash of green to a soft pink background; contrast can be used to achieve restrained emphasis. When only the necessary elements are being used in your graphic design, their relationships become obvious. Even in a layout's simplicity, clarity of tone and message is made possible by juxtaposition.

Below: Black and white is often used to create subtle contrast and minimalistic designs.

BALANCE

Many of the terms used in this book are not exclusive to graphic design (for example, proximity). We should read these broadly applied words differently in a book about graphic design but their root meanings remain. Balance is another term we can contextualize slightly for our purposes.

The word 'balance' is used so often that it is not hard to see how it can refer to a two-dimensional expression of what we experience in the physical world: a scale, standing on one foot, learning to ride a bike. When all the pieces are in the right relationship, balance is achieved.

Note: Balance in graphic design is quite a large topic; one to explore further in the next chapter (see page 52).

WHAT IS BALANCE?

Balance manages the distribution of weight between graphic elements. It requires the sensitive positioning of differently weighted objects in a way that achieves equilibrium. Visually, a 'heavier' element might be larger. It might be a stronger colour (see 'Contrast' on page 38, and the

chapter on 'The Right Colour',
page 76). It may also apply
to proximity; several
elements are grouped
closely together (see
'Proximity' on page 19).
When the distribution of
weight is 'off', the design
feels 'off' to the viewer,
which compromises the
design's purpose.

RACHELPICKWEDDINGS.COM
604 555 6267
INFO@RACHELPICKWEDDINGS.COM
VANCOUVER, BC

Above: This business card uses proximity to balance
two main elements: logo and text.

Less is More

It's worth making a note on intentionally diminishing an element in order to achieve balance.
Sometimes a graphic that seems as though it should be strong could compromise the whole of
the design. Logo design is a good illustration of this conundrum. In designing a logo for a client,
you may be tempted to make the logo (the icon or graphic) and the wordmark (the text or
name of the business) of equal visual weight.

Above: Contrasting the size of the logo and the text in the right-hand image here creates a stronger logo.

This might be too evenly weighted and lack texture. Think of a logo as you would a poster, and look for ways to offset the graphics to include some contrast and variation in the arrangement. Weakening one part will strengthen the whole.

ACHIEVING BALANCE

Balance is achieved through counterbalance. A graphic element is offset by an opposing element that keeps the visual weight and emphasis in check. Here are some ways graphic designers work towards compositional balance.

Quick Tip

The best way to assess whether or not your mini composition is graphically balanced is to print off as many renditions as you can, post them on the wall, and carefully pay attention to your intuitive response to each. Discard the ones you know are weak, and narrow down your options to the ones you feel you can refine.

Balance and the Grid

While much of balance is recognized by how it feels intuitively, it is actually achieved with planning and structure (see the section on grids in the 'Spatial Awareness' chapter, page 56). Spatially arranging elements in balance is made possible when an underlying structure, a grid, directs the placement of objects.

Humans respond to order, and grids provide a proportional and therefore aesthetically comfortable foundation.

Quick Tip

Grids are great for arranging elements spatially, but they're also indispensible for projects involving, or with the potential to involve, other designers. Another designer can utilize your grid and thus maintain the integrity of your design.

Below: It can been seen here how useful the grid is in creating an impactful design.

Weight and Messaging

If an advertisement for an exciting sale does not have 'Sale!' as the most weighted visual, it is not immediately clear what the advertisement is for, and the chances of it being overlooked by the target audience are high. The balance achieved here is a balance of hierarchy. For the most important piece of information to be weaker than or on a par with secondary and tertiary levels of information (date, time and so on), the message is not balanced.

Below: An advertisement will be glanced at quickly, so your message must be immediately clear.

SPECTACULAR SEAT SALE
3 days only. Ends August 3.

Choose from a great selection of destinations like New York City, Montreal, Sydney, Cape Town, Munich, and Zurich, among others, then save on your flight when you book by August 5, 2015.

SPECTACULAR
SEAT SALE
3 days only. Ends August 3.

Choose from a great selection of destinations like New York City, Montreal, Sydney, Cape Town, Munich, and Zurich, among others, then save on your flight when you book by August 5, 2015.

Types of Balance

This topic will be outlined in full in the next chapter but as a brief primer, consider symmetry and asymmetry as two arrangements you can use to balance your compositions. They are relatively simple to employ and relate to alignment, above.

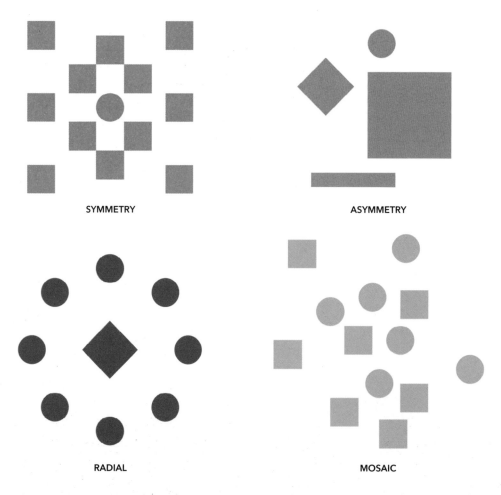

SYMMETRY

ASYMMETRY

RADIAL

MOSAIC

Above: Symmetry and asymmetry are easy to employ and can add balance.

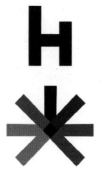

Above: This logo for a consultancy group utilizes both the rectilinear shapes and heavy line to convey an air of strength.

Weight for Shapes and Lines

Squares are understood to be strong shapes, and capable of eliciting great visual power. Thick lines are more visible than thin lines.

Weight and Size

Typically, the larger an element, the stronger it is, and the more necessary it is to assess its dominance in your layout. Counter-balancing a large element can be done by positioning a smaller element with similar strength in close enough proximity for the relationship to be evident.

PRINCIPLES INTO PRACTICE

You can probably see how these building blocks, these principles, overlap slightly in purpose and effect. Using them together is the key to good graphic design. No single building block is sufficient without the others. Simply relying on repetition to bring visual strength to a design, without considering contrast, results in a monotonous composition without focus or messaging power.

Practise seeing elements in terms of their proximity to one another. Practise seeing how elements can be aligned to bring order to your design. Intentionally look for graphic themes that could be tastefully repeated to enhance your message's power. Be keenly aware of hierarchical blandness, and how contrast could provide needed distinction. And finally, practise seeing imbalance (and read more about it in the next chapter).

Above: This cover for a research journal uses small text to offset the size of the fruit fly, an otherwise very small creature.

SPATIAL AWARENESS

GETTING SPACING RIGHT

When we view graphic design, we typically pay attention to the main subject in a layout – the primary message. That's the point of design, after all: to communicate clearly. However, designers must visually consider not only the subject, but the space around, behind and beside it.

COMPOSITION

This chapter focuses on spatial awareness. That is, understanding how to use the space of your artboard to best communicate your message. It is an important skill necessary in achieving visual balance and harmony, two founding elements of graphic design.

Below: The minimalistic approach to space in this book is used effectively.

A term that is used frequently in this section is 'composition'. It is defined as the overall placement of graphic elements on your artboard. A strong composition is balanced and harmonious – its graphic elements are in proper proximity to each other, are aligned according to a structure, and employ repetition and contrast to ensure the message is conveyed clearly and dynamically.

You have opened a new file, and staring back at you is a blank sheet of paper, as it were. The dreaded blank canvas! Where do you start?

Below and Left: These images from the same book show differently sized elements according to the same master layout.

GRID SYSTEMS

Despite appearances, canvases are never truly blank. Neither are artboards. A grid – a structure – is invisible but present; it's the underlying foundation of every successful composition.

Whether for web or print, your artboard can be divided into evenly spaced horizontal rows and vertical columns. Together, these intersecting lines provide rules along which text and images can be aligned. A grid does not guarantee a successful design, but it is an essential element in every successful design.

Below: Images and text can be aligned using a grid.

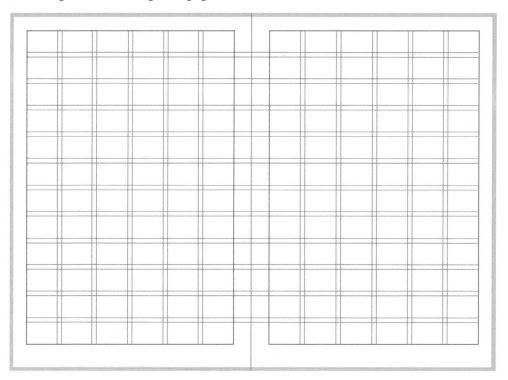

WHAT DOES A GRID ACHIEVE?

Humans subconsciously find grids visually satisfying.
Here are some practical benefits of grid systems:

- **Essential for usability**: Grids ensure that information is accessible, page to page. Users or readers expect repeated elements, such as a menu bar or page numbers, to be located in the same spot on each page.

- **Time-efficiency**: Blindly adjusting your layout until it feels right could exceed your budget for a client. Grids can accelerate the process and keep you from stalling when faced with otherwise endless layout possibilities.

Below: Using a grid will allow you to put key elements, such as page numbers and titles, in the same places on each page, so that the design is easy to follow.

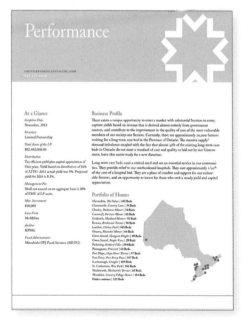

Quick Tip

As many a painter could tell you, a blank canvas can be daunting. Using a grid gives you a place to start. The tips in this book are not just about how to design well, but also about how to work well.

Above: The grid can also be useful when creating a logo. Keeping consistency between designs is vital for brand image.

- ▷ **Anchor the elements of a logo:** This enables other designers to use your file, which is important in applying a brand consistently across various media and over months or years, especially for in-house design departments working with multiple designers.

- ▷ **Define visual themes:** A classically centred layout is appropriate for an invitation to a baroque choral performance but not a release party for an electronica album. The spatial relationships of elements can create an overall tone.

Below: Here is an example of a classically centred layout used well for an invitation.

Kathryn Williams
AND
Martin Carter

INVITE YOU TO ATTEND THEIR
MARRIAGE
ON SATURDAY, OCTOBER 10TH, 2017
AT 5 O'CLOCK IN THE AFTERNOON
AND JOIN THEM IN CELEBRATION

LOREM HOTEL
ORLANDO, FLORIDA

TO BE FOLLOWED BY DINNER,
DRINKS AND DANCING

SIZE AND PROPORTION

Grids are calculated according to the proportions of your artboard, so determine what size serves the content early in the process. It will ground your project from the start.

Proportion and Content

How proportion and scale pertain to grid systems needs to be understood. Let's use an art book featuring large paintings as an example.

(1) The length-width proportions of the art book should echo those of the paintings. The paintings are 90 x 120 cm (standard canvas size). Scaled down by three gives us 30 x 40 cm, perfect for a large art book. Adding 20 mm margins around the top, bottom and sides makes the document 320 x 420 mm. From here, a grid of 10 mm square units is established.

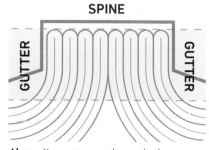

SPINE

GUTTER   GUTTER

Above: You must remember to check that the gutter is large enough.

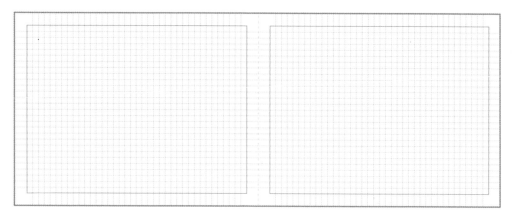

Step 1. A grid is created with the content in mind.

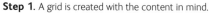

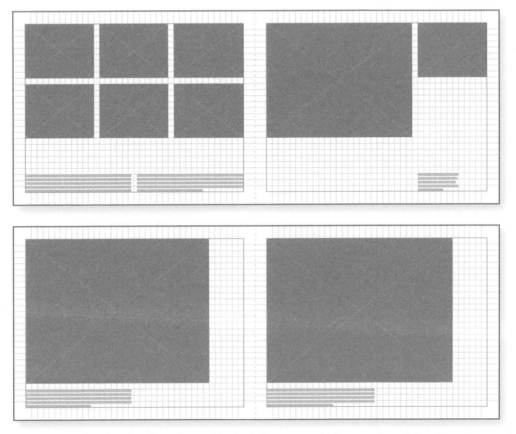

Step 2. Using grids such as these for an illustrated book will allow you to make the most of an artist's work.

② This grid provides a foundation on which to arrange the images and corresponding text. Scaling the paintings according to their proportions can now be reinforced by the book itself and properly honour the artist's works.

Budgets

Projects are usually limited by budget restraints. You may only afford to print on standard ISO-sized sheets. Every restraint must be seen as a guide. At the very least, it means one less decision to make.

Proportion and Web Design

Web design is relatively young, but note how dramatically spatial awareness has progressed online. In utilizing the same principles traditionally used in fine art and printing, web design has progressed to sophisticated compositions that are both attractive and user-friendly.

Right: The grid for this website provides information to enable a block of text to be shortened and thus more readable for users.

Quick Tip

Having text span the entire width of your browser is very difficult to read. The width of the text can also be limited by browser constraints and the responsive nature of a site. Use your grid to limit your text frames to readable lengths.

Above: The rule of thirds is a classic rule for a reason: it creates energy and interest in an image.

TYPES OF GRIDS

Grids have an important place in the history of graphic design, fine art, mathematics, architecture and science. Here are three grids that have been used throughout history.

The Rule of Thirds

This grid divides an artboard into thirds. Look at landscape photography. Are horizons positioned directly in the middle of a frame? You probably see more sky (or land) in two thirds of the composition. Try grouping elements in the same way and see how this impacts your layout.

The Golden Rectangle/Ratio

The Golden Rectangle is produced when you make a square from one end of your rectangular artboard. The resulting smaller rectangle can be divided further.

The Fibonacci Spiral

Connected to the Golden Ratio is the Fibonacci Spiral, a numerical sequence progressing by the sum of the previous pair. The diagram illustrates how the sequence (1, 1, 2, 3, 5, 8, 13 ...) is graphically expressed. The resulting lines become your grid system.

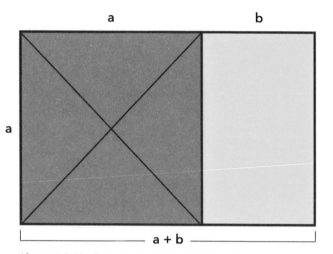

Above: A Golden Rectangle is said to be pleasing to the eye.

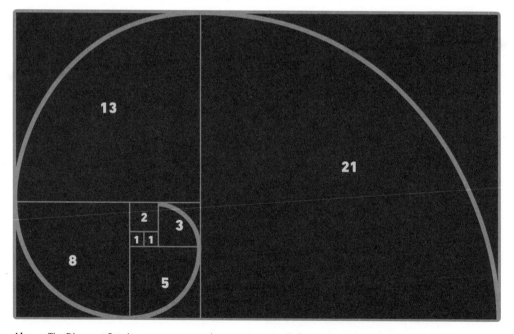

Above: The Fibonacci Spiral is an interesting grid system to use and often makes eye-catching final designs.

BRINGING BALANCE TO A PAGE

Spatial awareness helps a designer achieve visual balance – graphic elements are each given an appropriate amount of strength. A balanced page does not mean that every graphic element shares the same emphasis – hierarchy of messaging always matters – but it does mean that a design is viewed as a whole.

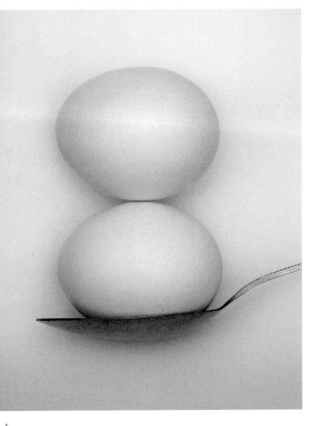

Below: Graphic designers can employ balance and harmony into photographic compositions and lighting.

TYPES OF BALANCE

Balance relies on grids. The following sections on balance and harmony assume you are employing grids in your layouts.

Balance is achieved in four main ways. Symmetrical balance and asymmetrical balance are the two most common methods. Radial and mosaic balance are also effective.

Quick Tip

Classic is not boring. Many a dynamic design has employed symmetry to communicate with clarity and strength. Ceremonial art and architecture, for example, are often symmetrical and aesthetically powerful.

Symmetrical Balance

Symmetry simply means that two elements with the same visual weight are positioned on either side of a central axis. It conveys a classic, formal tone.

Above: Architecture and nature can be a great source of inspiration to designers.

Left: Symmetrical designs are used frequently because they are a great way of balancing a page.

Above: Using asymmetrical balance is a great way to get the attention of a viewer.

Above: Radial balance is often used when lots of components connect to, or strengthen, a key message.

Above: It is important to make sure your message is clear when using mosaic balance.

Asymmetrical Balance

When elements of different visual weight and emphasis are skilfully placed in an uneven way, the design is asymmetrically balanced. Asymmetrical balance appears casual and informal, and generates a sense of movement and energy.

Radial Balance

Radial balance looks like what it suggests: components arranged radially around a single focal point. The centre is the focus of the message, because all secondary elements extend from it.

Mosaic Balance

Without any obvious point of focus, mosaic balance is difficult to recognize initially; it looks as though the pieces have been positioned at random. But this is not the case. There may not be a clear hierarchy, but visually the composition is unified.

SEEING BALANCE

Test your design by stepping back and paying close attention to how your eye travels across the space. Think about the following three points:

Counterbalance

Is one object demanding too much attention? One aspect of balance is obviously counterbalance. A teeter-totter needs two opposing weights to operate properly.

Quick Tip

After incrementally nudging things to the right, the left, up or down, request feedback from colleagues if possible. Their assessment will provide the fresh perspective needed in order to refine.

A strong graphic offset by a secondary one produces layouts that are visually (and conceptually) effective.

Visual Path

To what area of your artboard is your eye drawn to first? Second? Has your design met its messaging objective? Our eyes follow paths of graphic emphasis, and balance ensures an viewer is guided correctly through the information.

Distraction

Where is the visual weight situated? Are intersecting lines or strong contrasting shapes or colours distracting you from the project's focus? Once identified, you know the problems left to resolve.

Above: The dark blur is removed from the right image, making the overall design more effective.

BRINGING HARMONY TO A PAGE

Dictionary entries for the word 'harmony' include synonyms such as 'unity', 'compatibility' and 'co-operation'. Applied to graphic design, harmony describes the use of similar elements, which by nature of their commonality, establish a graphic theme and work together successfully.

WHAT IS HARMONY IN GRAPHIC DESIGN?

In music, harmony is a combination of notes which, when played together, sound pleasant to our ears. Likewise, a harmonious layout in graphic design is composed of similar elements that are visually pleasing.

BALANCE

Left: A balanced design is a type of harmonious design; here you can see the differences between them.

HARMONY

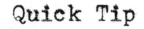

Quick Tip

Yes, harmony concerns spatial arrangements of graphic elements, but it also concerns how you choose and adjust the elements themselves. A colour palette of analogous colours (see page 84) or repeating the same shape are two simple ways to achieve visual harmony.

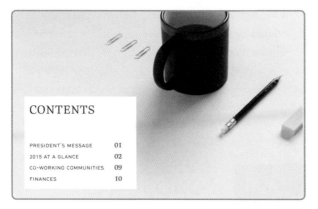

Above: The mug in the top image here is uncomfortable on the eye. With just a few small changes, the design is much more pleasing.

This Sounds a Lot Like Balance

Let's clarify the difference between harmony and balance:

- **Balance:** This refers to different graphic elements working together because of their difference. They counterbalance each other, generating a pleasing tension.

- **Harmony:** This refers to similar elements working with each other because of their similarities.

- **Harmony is a larger category:** Balance resides within this category. You cannot have a harmonious design that is not balanced.

Quick Tip

Ask yourself, does everything feel as though it belongs? If not, identify what your eye is landing on. Does it need to be removed? Or just moved? Should it share more graphic traits with surrounding elements?

HARMONY AND BLANDNESS

Harmony can, if not scrutinized, make for visually uninteresting design. Too much sameness is dull. Each design element needs to be distinct enough to hold interest, but unified so as not to confuse the viewer. How can you achieve harmony without blandness?

HARMONY NEEDS CONTRAST

By definition, contrast should contradict harmony. But contrasting elements can save a harmonious design from being boring. In this way, contrast is inherently a part of harmony.

Quick Tip

A harmonious design in need of contrast? Turn to building blocks such as repetition, contrast or colour. You can also add texture by playing with line weights and typefaces. Design should be unified, but not at the cost of visual interest.

HARMONY NEEDS CONCEPTUAL STRENGTH

Your design is not just graphic bits on an artboard. Graphic design is smart. It includes metaphors, visual puns, irony, cultural and historical references, and so on. Incorporating a clever device can keep a harmonious design from being visually drab.

Left: The lowercase 'g' in this branding/titling project becomes a lamp kept lit through the legacy of giving for this non-profit initiative.

WHITE SPACE

White space is sometimes referred to as negative space. But 'negative' is an unfortunate association. Does the phrase 'less is more' sound familiar? With practice, using fewer elements can actually increase the power of your design.

WHAT IS WHITE SPACE?

White space is any area with no content. It is the space between elements. And it is not always white. It can be a colour or a part of an image with no informative detail – a vast expanse of sky, for example. So, how can a space with no content be of any use?

What Does White Space Achieve?

The answer lies in the problems it solves.

Below: White space such as sky can be useful in a design.

◐ **Reprieve:** Busy layouts tire our eyes, and our senses can be overwhelmed. White space provides reprieve for the eye.

◐ **Prioritizing:** Some designs are packed with graphics that have little communications value. White space demands that messaging priorities are clear. If an element has no purpose, it is distracting clutter.

Above: Removing unnecessary elements in a design will often strengthen it.

◐ **Focus:** White space isolating a singular element can build focus. It can strengthen a message by encouraging viewers to focus on fewer elements.

Right: If there is not enough white space, information is often lost, sometimes physically on the page, or if a viewer is not able to take everything in.

Confidence: A simplified design can imply that a client does not feel compelled by its competition to be louder or bolder in order to be valued in the marketplace. Self-assured designs can exude reliability.

Legibility: In regards to typography, white space can make densely packed text more legible. Decreasing the size of a font and increasing the space between lines of text provides breathing space for words.

> **3 MAY. BISTRITZ.** Left Mu 1st May, arriving at Vienna should have arrived at 6:46, late. Buda-Pesth seems a w the glimpse which I got of i little I could walk through t very far from the station, as would start as near the corr impression I had was that w and entering the East; the n bridges over the Danube, w width and depth, took us ar Turkish rule.
>
> We left in pretty good time, to Klausenburgh. Here I sto Hotel Royale. I had for dinr

> **3 MAY. BISTRITZ.** Left Mu 1st May, arriving at Vienna should have arrived at 6:46, late. Buda-Pesth seems a w the glimpse which I got of i little I could walk through t very far from the station, as would start as near the corr impression I had was that w and entering the East; the n bridges over the Danube, w width and depth, took us ar Turkish rule.

Above: It is much easier to read text that has space between the lines.

Simplicity: White space says 'easy to use'. For some projects, this could be the impression that you want to convey.

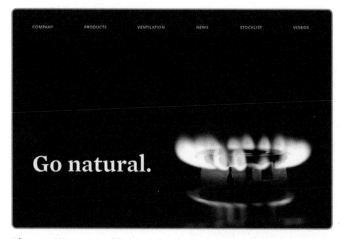

COMPANY   PRODUCTS   VENTILATION   NEWS   STOCKLIST   VIDEOS

Go natural.

Quick Tip

Too much white space can be forgettable. Turn to the building blocks discussed in the first chapter for help (see page 16). Playing with proximity or grouping, for example, can clear up space and provide emphasis.

Above: White space, or 'black space' as the case may be, clarifies options for users and sells a supposedly non-intimidating product.

WHITE SPACE IS AN ELEMENT

Layouts with fewer elements only look easier to design. The challenge is rooted in mistakenly seeing white space as passive – as a non-element. Remember, underlying every artboard is a grid (see page 56). Use it to see white space as a graphic – an object to shape and enhance your design.

Below: Framing a photograph with ample white space provides space for content, but be sure your content echoes the aesthetic quality of the photograph.

Roost presents
DIY Furniture Refresh
Monday 7pm on CTV

Less is More

Luxury brands prefer ample white space in advertisements. Conversely, discount brands pack a page or screen with graphics. This approach is not directly related to saving on printing costs. Rather, a full page conveys 'more for less' to a customer, a strategy based on extensive demographic and market research.

WHITE SPACE AND MINIMALISM

White space is associated with minimalism (mid-20th century), which focused on stripping design to essentials and rejecting ornamentation. Minimalism is beautiful but can be austere. Unless your project is conceptually strengthened by a nod to this era, do not be dissuaded from modest flourish.

Think of white space as a strength that serves the rest of the graphic elements rather than as a passive player in your design process. It can be an active element in your compositions.

Quick Tip

Minimal design need not be cold. It can be inviting. Look to Japanese design and architecture and note how white space can be warm and hospitable.

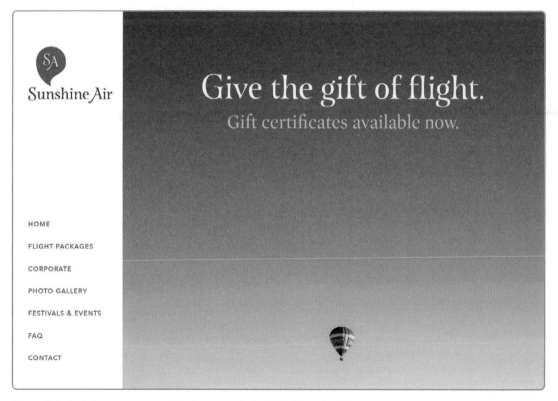

Above: This simple home page uses minimalism to emphasize sky, heights, simplicity, peace.

THE RIGHT COLOUR

THE IMPORTANCE OF GETTING COLOUR RIGHT

Colour is not just about making design look pretty. It is a serious and incredibly important design element. Colour is a language. It affects us all deeply. The reason lies in its power to persuade and its capacity to capture emotion. A basic understanding of colour theory and how to use it infuses your work with sophistication and confidence.

COLOUR AND COMMUNICATION

If you're ever unsure about how important colour is to design, consider that marketing agencies invest considerable amounts into researching demographics and colour's effect on consumers. Colour forecasting experts are often consulted by various industries as they work to attract a specific audience.

In graphic design, a wrong colour combination compromises a design by communicating a tone contrary to the project's end goal. This is why choosing your favourite colour is not an option. You need to be objective about all aesthetic decisions you make for a client – and colour is no different. Green is our favourite colour. Blue may be yours. But graphic design is not about us. It's about communication.

Below: A main feature of this booklet is its use of vibrant colour, providing the necessary energy and enthusiasm required by the client. Two more pages can be seen below.

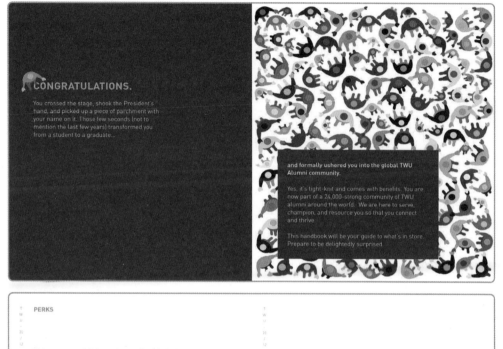

THE INTRINSIC VALUE OF DIFFERENT COLOURS

Colours can hold a great deal of meaning. The strong associations, emotions and themes connected to specific colours confirm that they're often symbolic. Making sure that colour says the right thing to the right person is vital.

COLOUR AND CULTURE

Yellow can represent prestige in Africa but sadness in Greece. In South America, green is associated with death, but in the Middle East, it means luck. Graphic designers must consider culture when brainstorming colour schemes for a client.

Colours and their Significance

The abbreviated list below underlines the importance of research, understanding your audience or viewer, and of being open to associations different from those of your own.

- **Blue**: Peace, professionalism, honour, melancholia, depth, communication or conservatism. In Mexico, blue symbolizes bereavement.

- **Red**: Heat, love, anger, danger, strength or socialism. In Eastern cultures, red means luck and prosperity.

Yellow: Optimism, joy, cowardice or intellect. Yellow aids in releasing serotonin in the brain. It is attention-grabbing.

Green: Optimism, wealth, relaxation, freshness, nature or toxicity. In the Middle East, it can represent prestige, and in Africa, corruption.

White: Cleanliness, peace, innocence or sterility. In Asian cultures, white represents death and misfortune.

Black: Elegance, sophistication, formality, power, luxury, morbidity or secrecy. In some Asian cultures, black can mean both health and evil.

○ **Brown:** Comfort, organics, reliability, credibility or strength.

○ **Purple:** Royalty, wisdom, sophistication, artificiality, celebration, magic or creativity. Purple represents bereavement in Brazil.

○ **Orange:** Cheerfulness, joy, friendship, affordability, enthusiasm, stimulation, creativity, thirst or liberal politics.

○ **Pink:** Love, tenderness, physical feebleness, friendship or romance. We consider pink feminine, but in Belgium, it is used for boys.

THE COLOUR WHEEL

Sir Isaac Newton's colour wheel organizes 12 root colours – the 12 purest, brightest colours. These root colours represent countless incremental hues, which together complete the spectrum we are physically capable of seeing.

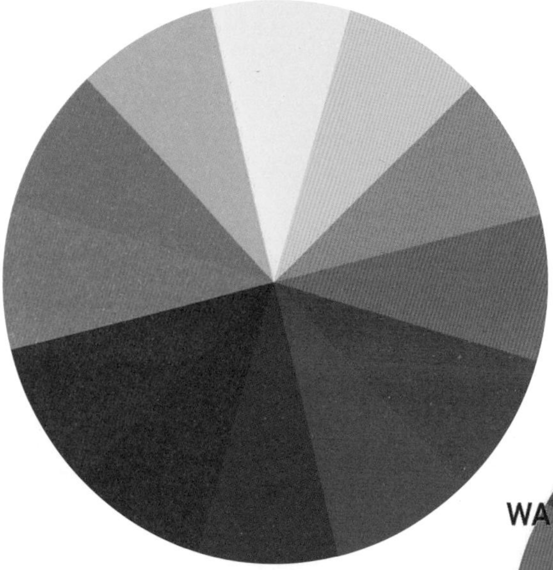

Above: The colour wheel collates the 12 purest colours.

BASIC TERMS DEFINED

Here we look at the colour wheel and how it works.

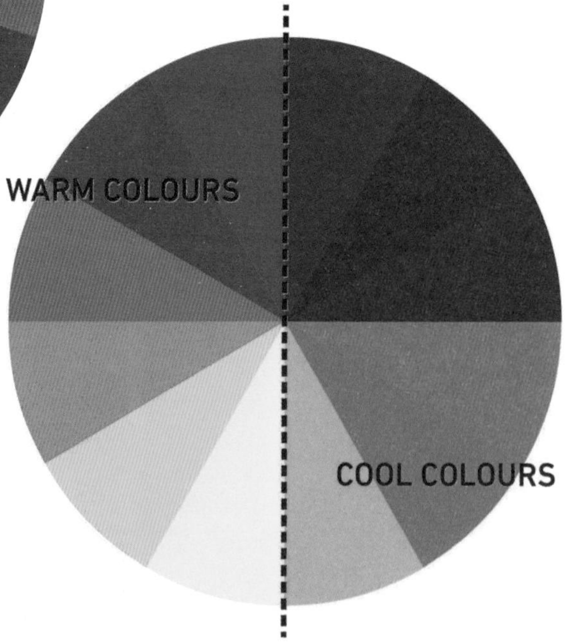

WARM COLOURS

COOL COLOURS

Colour

The first word to define is the most obvious. Colour and hue are used interchangeably, both referring to pigmentation.

Warm and Cool Colours

Around the colour wheel, warm colours span from red-violet to yellow, and are effective in motivating response. Cool colours rotate around the opposite side (purples to greens), and have soothing, calming effects.

Above: Warm colours motivate and excite, while cool colours are more likely to evoke a more logical, calm response.

WORLD-LEADING TO WIN US TRIALS 200M FINAL

Justin Gatlin became the fifth-fastest 200m runne
he won Sunday's final at the American Athletics.

THE 33-YEAR-OLD AMERICAN, who has served two doping bans, recorde
seconds in Oregon. It bettered the 19.68 secs he ran in May which, at that s
in the world. Gatlin has been the dominant sprinter in 2015, having

Value, Tints and Shades

Value refers to how light or dark a hue is. Adding white creates a tint and adding black makes a shade.

Left: Adding black to this background green creates a shade that contrasts well with the bright pink.

Below: Here you can see a scale of tints and shades.

| + WHITE = TINT | + BLACK = SHADE |

Tone

A hue's tone is adjusted by adding grey. Toning down a colour is an effective way of making root colours more usable for two reasons. Firstly, the bright colour wheel is not represented naturally in our world, and tones better reflect our surroundings. Secondly, bright colours can tire the eye, and adding grey takes the edge off.

+ GREY = TONE

Above: Adding grey can soften a bright colour and create a new tone.

Chroma

Chroma is used to describe a colour's purity. The varying factor is how much of the hue's complement (see below) is present. The colour in the middle of the scale is considered neutral, meaning it is lacking in hue.

Below: A colour's purity is described as its chroma.

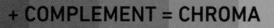

+ COMPLEMENT = CHROMA

DEFINING AND USING THE COLOUR WHEEL

The colour wheel demonstrates the relationships between our 12 root colours and is used in all visual disciplines, in mathematics, science and psychology.

Primary, Secondary and Tertiary Colours

The colour wheel's founding colours (red, blue and yellow) are primary, because they cannot be produced by mixing any pigments. In fact, all other colours are products of mixing these three, and doing so produces three secondary colours. Were you then to mix a primary and secondary colour, you would get tertiary hues: yellow-orange, red-orange, red-purple, blue-purple, blue-green and yellow-green.

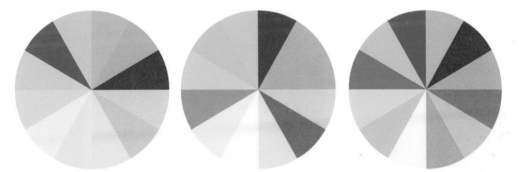

Above: When the primary colours (left) are mixed, they produce the secondary colours (middle).

Above: Primary and secondary colours together make tertiary colours.

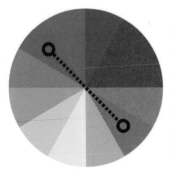

Complementary Colours

Complementary colours sit directly opposite each other on the colour wheel. When two complements are mixed together, they produce a neutral grey.

Above: Colours on the wheel that are opposite each other are called complementary colours.

Above: Christmas colours – green and red – are complementary.

Analogous Colours

Any three colours located next to each other on the colour wheel are analogous.
Schemes inspired by nature are often analogous.

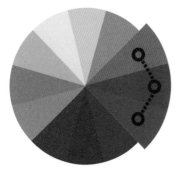

BANISH CLUTTER

How to Organize
Every Room in Your Home   by Tom Bonnett

Our organizational home tour starts in the living room, which is w
ing, hanging out, and happiest memory-making takes place. Here, y
tive, clear-eyed view of your clutter and how it impacts your every
solidating all of your electronics in one custom cabinet and use lin

Above: Colours that are located next to each other on the
wheel are sometimes used together. They are analogous colours.

Above: Use strong hues of your
colours to help establish hierarchies.

Monochromatic Colours

Monochromatic
schemes are not
found on the standard
colour wheel because
they are comprised
of tints and shades
of a single hue.

Left: It is possible to
compose a photograph
based on a single
colour, the variations
of which provide depth
and interest.

Triadic Colours

A triadic colour scheme is any three colours at equal distance from each other on the colour wheel. These combinations are excellent for providing unified contrast.

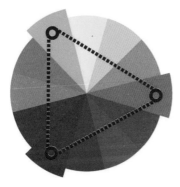

Above: Triadic colours such as the ones indicated here provide the best contrast.

Left: The colour wheel is very useful in the development of brand colours. This brand's founding palette is triadic based on the dark blue.

Tetradic Colours

Tetradic colour schemes are comprised of two complementing pairs.

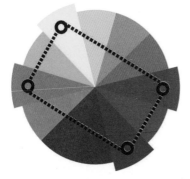

Above: Tetradic colour schemes tend to be very vibrant and care must be taken to make sure the scheme does not become jarring.

THE MEANING OF COLOUR

Next time you're out and about, make a note of product packaging, building signage and window displays. What do you find most appealing? What repels you? Colour impresses upon us without us even noticing.

COLOUR AND PURPOSE

Imagine you are designing a logo for a financial services bureau. When you conduct your research, you notice that many competing brands feature blue. It may be an indication that blue is the most effective colour, and you should consider using it. Or it might mean that this office needs to stand out – that something unconventional is in order. If available, consult marketing expertise for guidance.

Red

Because red can rouse a sense of urgency and energy, it is successful in promoting sales and the entertainment industry (Netflix, Nintendo, Virgin). It is also used for Valentine's Day, representing love and passion.

HOW WE ENVISION
Mobile Enterprise

LEARN MORE
ABOUT **PORTAL**

Blue

As a colour people trust, blue is often used to represent financial services and technologies. Consider Barclays, RBS, IBM and PayPal. But it is an unappetizing choice for promoting food-related products.

Yellow

Yellow gets our attention. It's excitable and happy. For this reason, it is used for emergency services and McDonald's.

Quick Tip

Yellow is the first colour the brain registers. Why else would emergency services use it? It does the job – it catches your eye fast.

Orange

Also attention-grabbing, orange is a popular choice when promoting affordable goods. It is fun, conveys enthusiasm, creativity and active living, and attracts children (Nickelodeon, Halloween, and drinks such as Fanta). It also represents liberal politics.

Green

Green symbolizes nature and is used in promoting eco-friendly and fair-trade initiatives, and freshness (Waitrose). It is also an effective colour in isolation, in that it has the capacity to stand out as unusual, and therefore as memorable.

FOOD

Best Farm-to-Table Restaurants in London
By Christie Reed

Black

Black is formal and glamorous. This makes it a solid option for luxury goods – products conveying an air of seriousness and exclusivity.

Purple

Purple's association with elegance, sophistication, wealth and royalty make it a popular choice in marketing anti-ageing products and decadent chocolate (Cadbury). Brands like Premier Inn have used the colour successfully to represent luxury.

Quick Tip

Be careful – purple can sometimes be interpreted as goofy and should be supplemented by grounding colours and/or tints and shades.

Brown

Brown is a colour that many people do not notice elicits a sense of dependability and warmth. UPS is one of the most popular brands to stand on this assumption.

Pink

Pink is typically reserved for marketing to girls (Barbie, Roxy) and has become symbolic in its representation of breast cancer awareness.

CREATING A COLOUR PALETTE

Now you've gained a nit of background knowledge of colour theory and have an appreciation for the importance of colour, how do you create a palette?

Above: The combination of gold and green is unusual, but works well here.

Brainstorm

One popular method designers use to choose colours is to create a collage of inspiring images from graphic design, architecture, interior design, fashion, photography, food styling, fine art and so on. Such a compilation of pictures often reveals colour themes.

THE CREATIVE PROCESS OF COLOUR SELECTION

Colour theory has a firm foundation in science, but colour selection should be creative too. Take risks and experiment – you will encounter some surprising combinations.

Before the fun, return to your design brief. Similar to how white space can intimidate, the endless spectrum of colours can overwhelm. Remember, there is always a base from which to step: the design's message.

This sample mood board (right) of found imagery provided a start for a palette for a photographer's brand.

Other ways to brainstorm include pulling out your paints, starting an online library of images (try Pinterest), strolling through nature, a vegetable market, antique toy store, art gallery, bookshop and so on. Colour is everywhere.

Left & Above: Mood boards can be used as inspiration for projects.

Quick Tip

Graphic themes and typefaces can be decided upon with the help of mood boards. The board to the left of found imagery guided many design elements in a book of poetry. See also the section on selecting the right typography pages 106–34.

TRADITIONAL COLOUR THEORY APPLIED

Let's return to the colour combinations derived from the colour wheel. They provide a solid method of interpreting your brainstorming into real swatches usable for both print and web.

Complementary Colours

Complements are dynamic – perhaps too much so. Adjusting tints and shades generates transitional hues to make a more functional set of swatches. In the example shown, the complements are flanked by supporting swatches, useful in secondary headings, graphics and backgrounds.

Above: A colour palette can be made by adjusting tints and shades.

Left: Sports logos and professional kits are a great place to find inspiration.

Quick Tip

If a project calls for punch, draw from professional sports for inspiration. Team logos, their uniforms and branding systems use strong complementary schemes, chosen for the energy they exude.

Split-complementary Colours

Split-complementary schemes are reliable and a quick way to experiment with less conventional combinations. The root colour of the scheme here is yellow, with the split complements in squares one and five.

Above: Split-complementary schemes like this one often have less obvious colour combinations.

Analogous Colours

Left alone, a trio of analogous colours may be too bright. Add several shades and tones to round out your options. Note here how the original trio has little variation in chroma; the messaging role of your palette can be hampered if there is too much similarity. By adjusting the shades and tones, we have viable options for different hierarchical needs.

Quick Tip

Limit the number of analogous colours in your scheme. Too many can render a composition muddy.

Above: Shades and tones can be added to analogous colour schemes to soften them.

Right:
This suite of logos uses a palette of analogous colours.

Monochromatic Colours

Monochromatic schemes are the most simple to build. By adjusting tone, tint and shade, it is difficult to go wrong. Their variations lie in the differing levels of strengths. If your project requires a strong hierarchical structure, monochromatic colours may not be the best option, leaving you looking for a contrasting hue for primary elements.

Above: You'll want to consider carefully which colour you choose if you decide to use a monochromatic colour scheme.

Triadic Colours

By choosing a triadic scheme, you may find that one hue is dominant. Depending on your messaging needs, the stronger hue could be supported well by the weaker ones, or it may need to be downplayed to achieve harmony. Try both options.

Above: Getting the balance of weaker and stronger colours that work well together in a triadic colour scheme is important.

Quick Tip

Adobe has given graphic designers a leg up with Colour Guide. Scroll down the pull-down menu to choose an option based on any root colour. But do not stop there. Always reassess default settings based on your project's specific needs.

Above: This pattern comprised of tetradic colours was based on a brand's signature blue.

Above: You must be careful when using a tetradic colour scheme as it can be too rich and hard to balance all of the colours.

Tetradic Colours

A rectangular tretrad provides visual interest, but it is tricky to balance and requires time to refine. If the four pure tones are competing with each other, tone down two or three of them.

CREATE YOUR OWN

The colour wheel is a solid place to start, but how can you push your palette further?

Grey, Black and White

There does exist a perfect neutral grey, but greys, blacks and whites are often flavoured slightly with a hue, which serves other colours in a palette well.

Right: Greys, blacks and whites are often tinged with a hue to allow them to fit in with the rest of a palette, as here.

Above: A palette can be completed by tan and cream colours, that unify the stronger hues.

Off-white, Beige and Tan

Black and white can be stark. Dark neutrals, tans and creams can unify a palette.

Use Photography

Base your palette on a photograph and let software do the groundwork for you. Import a photo into InDesign and select the Colour Theme Tool (under Eyedropper). Then click the photo. A bar of swatches presents options for brightness and tone. Choose a set and add it to your main Swatches palette or the Creative Cloud library to be refined (always be critical of the combinations your computer generates).

Quick Tip

Have you heard of Adobe Colour? This website can help you develop sophisticated palettes, and it exports your final selection to Adobe's CC suite. You can also view palettes developed by other designers. See pages 198–200 for more on Adobe.

Marshmallow Palette

Right: A quick way to generate a colour scheme is to base it on a photograph.

CHOOSING COLOUR FOR PRINT

The exercise of choosing colours is the same whether designing for print or screen. In fact, many communications suites include both printed and web components and share colour palettes. But picking colours based on how they look on a monitor is not wise, and this section explains why.

When working with your file on a screen, you are viewing projected light. But when printed, you see ink. Base your colour selection for a print on something that is printed.

PANTONE MATCHING SYSTEM

The Pantone Matching System (PMS) provides premixed inks, known as spot colours, and is certainly the most reliable way to ensure your project comes back from the printer looking great. Printed swatch books act like catalogues.

Right: Printed ink is a much more reliable source for choosing a colour than your computer screen.

Quick Tip

Peruse your PMS swatch books in natural light – it is the most honest. Diffused light, especially, illuminates surfaces evenly, so go through the books close to a window.

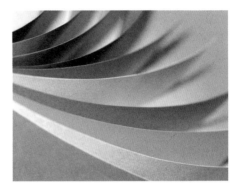

Quick Tip

Invest in relationships with sales representatives of paper mills and printers. They are experts in their fields and taking advantage of their knowledge is recommended, so never be afraid to ask 'stupid questions'.

Think About Paper

Even with PMS colour picking, other factors need to be considered when a project is sent to press. Pantone sells swatch books for coated paper and uncoated paper, enabling you to see how dramatically different the same PMS ink will print on papers with different surface treatments. Pick your paper with this in mind.

Above: Those who work on presses are artists themselves, trained to see detail, image resolution and colour balance that would be missed by most.

Think About Printers

Likewise, the printer you select could determine how your PMS colours are realized on paper. Printers are competing for your design project. One may provide a particularly competitive price – but do not settle until you have seen examples of their work.

Think About Location

If you are designing for a particular environment, visit the location at different times of day and in different weather. Will your design be visible?

Quick Tip

On a site visit, snap plenty of pictures and digitally compose your drafts on to them, to see how different colours interact with and impact the surrounding features.

Above: A quick mock-up of your design 'on location' is impressive to clients. They will see their project *in situ*, have an increased enthusiasm for their own initiative and leave the meeting optimistic and looking forward to the next stage of development.

CHOOSING COLOUR FOR SCREEN

We have covered the cultural, psychological and technical aspects of choosing colour for graphic design. But how colour functions in interactive media extends well beyond aesthetics to influencing behaviour. Choosing colours for interactivity is no small matter.

COLOUR AND USABILITY

How colour can both serve and direct a user is a major component of web design, and there are several factors to consider.

Brand Colours

Because most websites are expressions of a larger brand, incorporating brand colours is unavoidable. This could serve your design or pose a challenge. Regardless, utilize the palette to establish information hierarchy first. If needed, use colour theory to expand the palette to meet the design's communications goal.

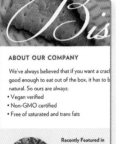

Quick Tip

If a palette is lacking in neutral tones, add some. Websites are served well by backgrounds that function as a stage for featured content.

Left: Sometimes white can be too stark and a tan colour can work better, as seen in the images here.

Contrast

Because monitors rely on projected light, contrast plays a primary role in how a website is viewed. Make sure areas of strong colours are grounded by tones or black or white. Avoid light, bright backgrounds behind text, because they compromise legibility.

Left: The dark background in the right image here makes the text much clearer.

Navigation

Use the bright colours in your palette for actionable items (buttons, menus, boxes, search fields and so on). They will be more visible and accessible when a user is prompted to perform a function. 'BUY NOW!' in red is more persuasive than 'BUY NOW!' in pink.

Right: Bright colours like the ones here are really good for menus, boxes, buttons and anything else that a user might interact with.

Below: Web-safe colours can be simple, but are safest when designing for old computers.

```
HTML  #00FFCC          HTML  #00FFFF
RGB   0 255 204        RGB   0 255 255
```

Colour Across Displays

The Web-safe colour system includes 216 colours that view the same regardless of monitor, operating system or browser. Although today's displays can render millions of colours, the system still has value when designing for the lowest common denominator of computers.

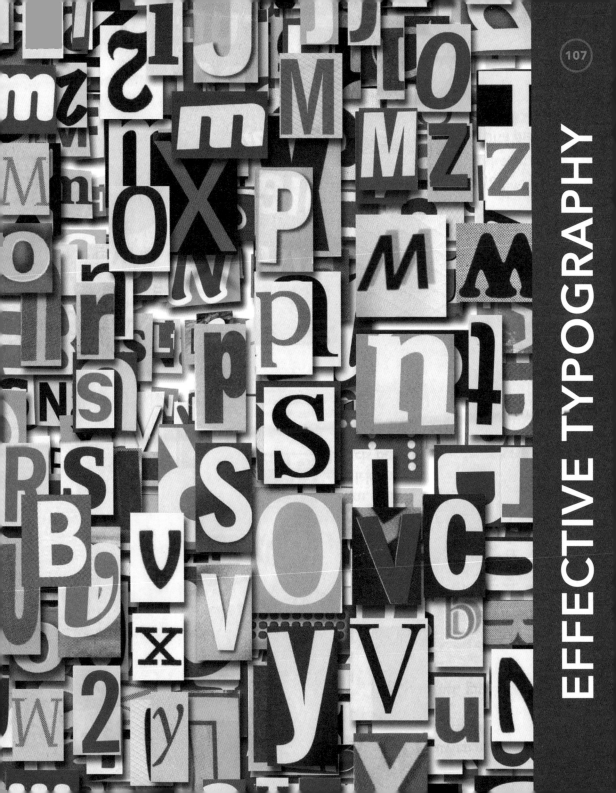

EFFECTIVE TYPOGRAPHY

USING TYPOGRAPHY

Good use of typography can make or break a design. It has the power to make something simple seem extraordinary, and something complicated easy to digest. This chapter will help you get over the basic but important typographic hurdles.

THE IMPORTANCE OF USING THE RIGHT TYPOGRAPHY

On a very basic level, any text that is legible and composed in a way that provides visual meaning in relation to its content is effective typography. It becomes the visual form of a language that can clearly communicate any type of information, narrative or instruction. It is a formal discipline with formal guidelines. These conventions are not rules, per se, because they can be subjective

Below: A blackletter font is a good example of decreased legibility in the letterforms because it is not commonly used for continuous text reading.

𝕿his font is harder to read continously when used in long form text because the letter= forms are difficult to dis= tinguish from each other.

and change according to context, medium and designer. Other factors should be considered, such as font size, spacing, emphasis, colour, legibility and readability, to name a few.

Conveying a Message

Well thought-out typography contributes to the overall impression and aesthetic of any project. It should translate and express its intended message, as well as maintain a harmonious relationship between the text and other elements in the design. Poor typography can bore, confuse or frustrate the audience by being difficult to read. The letterforms should be clear and easily distinguishable, as well as having an appropriate size for reading in a continuous flow. The lines on a page should also be structured in a manner that helps the eye read smoothly without too many interruptions.

Right: If a text is small it can be used for screen, book footnotes or anything that can be looked at up close. If a text is too big to read up close, it can easily be seen on a large poster, for example.

Quick Tip

Blackletter, also known as Gothic script, is part of the Latin writing system (alphabet) but it's a different calligraphic style that the character forms are based on. These are tall and narrow shapes formed by pointy, angular lines.

This font is easier to read because the letterforms are clear and the lines look crisp and sharp. There is good contrast and the size is adequate.

Above: Fonts that have distinguishable letterforms and good spacing, contrast and size are easier to read.

This font may have clear letterforms but it is now too small to read properly. This font may have clear letterforms but it is now too small to read properly. This font may have clear letterforms but it is now too small to Otooreet utat venotre dolorinisil utpat. Feugue dolobore erciliq uatumsan hent wis amcoriullan ulla commy nosto dunt ullaore erusto diam, quisi. Elenisl ute conum et ing et am dion henim velit, secte minciduip eriustrud dolutat do dignim vel iure vullan eugait dolore facillamcon exerat, vero od ting etuenit inusto dunt nibh euguer iustisim et dit, consequamet in eum nostis nosto corem dolessi sismodit am, sim in et, corecidunt am num irullumsa ndiat. Cum zzriuscita feum zzriit verosti onullup tatuerc illaor sit acil ipismod ionulla accumsan vel dolorper si er sit vel delendrem in hent del utem veniuscidunt non utat, quamet am alisi. Em vel del dolor summoloreet veliquis nulluptatie conse tat wismodi am dolorem zzriureet prat lut lor iustisl inim veliquam ex elisim amet at. quamcon hent ute consequat. Duis nullum zzriissis autpat. Ut venit wis ad dolobor ing ero dolore miri ut ebuer in ut autpatuero con ut iut at. Tie dunt wisis am, sim ero eum quisil lute consectem accum ad tat. Andre con eraestisit ut praessecte diam do consenim dolore commy niscinismod dolutate consenim quatem zzrii ea facil esed et, vulla commodo lortie commy nullam, quat. Onsequi ssecte eugait vel ercil eros ad tis nonsecte mincidunt ad modion ero digna faciduni ad min ex euismolendit verit adiatue ea facing endre enibh er sim nonumsandre mod min ex ea faciliupit ad dolorpe raessent am, eu feuis acilit wisl eugait wis nos adignis nonsed do exer am quatin vent ip et illaore eu feu facinis sequat, sum iniuscillam illa facilia aliquamet, vel utpat. Ugue facilis et lor suscitisim zzriusci blandrer sit iniureet ut aliquisl dolore vendrem quismol orperci ncincinis etue dignim verat ian vertisci blandrerate consod ea alaquate vero od dit dolore minim digna adiamco nullandre dolorperaese dolorpenit nulluptat. Cliquat. Im do elesequismod tie faccums andrercing ea feu facil ipit

Helvetica Regular 12pt — 100pt

This font size is too big to read comfortable from a ha held dista

CHOOSING A FONT

A typeface should be chosen with some sensitivity for the content of the text. As well as taking the subject into account, the target audience should also be influential. Will it be read by children or by adults? Will it be short text on a poster or a 500-page novel? The font should be coherent visually and also in meaning.

FINDING A BALANCE

Setting out to choose a typeface can be daunting due to the ever-growing and vast amount of choice that exists nowadays. A good approach would be to choose a font that would make sense within the context of the particular project, by matching the attributes of a typeface with the intended message. The font would have to reflect what it wanted to communicate – for example, by being visually subtle and delicate, or something robust and dominant.

SERIF CHARACTERS

SANS SERIF CHARACTERS

Above: Typefaces can be, very broadly, divided into serif or sans serif. Serif fonts have decorative flourishes at the ends of their strokes (circled red). This example shows a slab serif with flourishes that are flat and angular.

FLYER

Does this catch your attention?

Using bold and thick

condensed & mixed with other weights

Above: A flyer design would have bigger and bolder text to be able to stand out.

- **Bold:** A flyer might warrant a bold, thick sans serif in a larger point size to arrest attention.

- **Vibrant:** A modern cookbook with vibrant images might benefit from a mix of both serif and sans serif.

Think About Genre

All letterforms have their own character and history. Knowing when and why a font was made, and where it's been most used, can help with making a decision about whether it is appropriate.

Above: A medieval book can use a Caslon font because it has characteristics of a Dutch Baroque type, which gives it an older feel, without having to use Blackletter.

Another book might be written about the same era but based in Spain, and would be complemented by a typeface such as Pradell.

A historical book concerning the nineteenth century can work with a Dutch Baroque type such as a Caslon. The forms of Dutch Old Style typefaces were created mainly in the 17th century in the Netherlands. The shapes have contrast, a narrow proportion and a large x-height (see page 118).

Pradell is a Latin text family based on original *Spanish* 18th century type specimens & cut by Catalan punch cutter Eudald Pradell

*

Above: Pradell is a Spanish-inspired typeface that could work well for Catalan texts or for magazines looking for a serif font with a distinct delicate flair.

SIZE

Size plays an important role in typography, because it gives a design some visual consistency and optimizes the reading experience. Typography relies on size to be legible and readable enough for the different uses and roles in its design concept.

LEGIBILITY

To further understand how to properly manage size in typography, the designer must first understand the difference between legibility and readability. Legibility happens on a character level: the letterforms need to be distinguishable from each other and understood at a basic language level. For example, the character 'R' must not be confused with a 'B'.

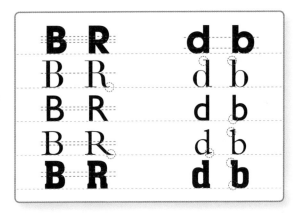

Above: You can see the distinct letterforms in these five different fonts. Some of them are more distinguishable in their shape, but other fonts have a more similar form, as in ITC Avant Garde.

Above: Historical and Impact have very similar letterforms that are difficult to distinguish from other characters. These therefore work better as heading styles rather than text fonts.

A font's legibility depends on its form and design for each writing system (such as in the Latin alphabet, the Greek script, Japanese, Cyrillic, and so on). The more letters the reader is able to recognize at once, the faster they can read, and this is why the characters must be precise in their distinctions.

READABILITY

Readability happens at a typographic level. The process of reading is dictated by the way letters are perceived, and these can look different depending on their scale. The details (serifs, sharp edges, angles and curves) of a typeface start to disappear the smaller the font gets. The text should not only have a clear contrast but also be an appropriate size to read. A poster allows for big type so that it can be read at a distance. A hand-held book can have much smaller type because it can be read up close.

Below: Bigger type works on posters or as large headlines on book covers or newspapers.

The letterforms are well designed but it has been blown up too big to read comfortably. It is above the average text size, which is 10-13pt (depending on the typeface).

This font is well designed but it has been cast too small to read comfortably. It is below the average text size, which is 10-13pt (depending on the typeface).

Minion Pro 7pt

Above: Type such as this needs to be read up close so it only works in smaller prints, such as books or pamphlets.

OPTICAL SIZE-SPECIFIC

Size adjustments are necessary in typefaces due to how our eyesight behaves. A page full of text is read differently in a newspaper than in a book or on a flyer. The latter might use bigger text because the information is bite-size and needs to catch immediate attention and be absorbed quickly. A flyer is a throwaway design piece, which is competing with other similar pieces, so the typography needs to be loud and to the point.

Magazines

On the other hand, a magazine page would use different font sizes for distinct purpose-specific designs: display fonts would be used for headlines; titling or subheading for subheaders; banner for advertisements; text for the main articles; and caption or small for the image captions.

Above: This magazine spread uses different font sizes for the headings, intro text, body copy, captions and sidebars.

Headline 36pt

Subtitle subtitle subtitle 24pt

The letterforms are well designed but it has been blown up too big to read comfortably. It is above the average text size, which is 10-13pt (depending on the typeface). Per sed magna ad eui blaor si.

Put lamet volore do conumsandrer am, commy nonse mincipit wisi.

Unt alis dui blan volorem quisse delestie vent wis nosto odiamcon henis at. Duisim zzriliq uipisisi.

Ed tie magna conullumsan erosto od ex exercinibh eugue magnibh erostin exeros nibh et prat. Ut wis niat lore magna aut am et am doluptat. Uscip el exer irit lorem accummolore tinci bla consed dit vero digna faccum dolobor sum zzril duis ad tatin etum volorem zzriure minciliquat il iriliquamet,

conulpute tionsenit iure vel ilis nonulla facip el ullandit nonsecte dolorpe raesent deliqui et veliqui blam quamcon ut ulla conullut do consenisi te molore te moloboreet lutpat autpat laorperilit lut la feuis niamcon sequis doloreet ing el ing eugiatummy nullam in er ad

Extract Extract Extract Extract 18pt

essequi blan ex ex ex et at, vent acipit lore venim delissit la aliquis dolorem doloreet iurem ipismodo odolore dolore doluptatem dolorpe rostissenis nisl ut la feu facidunt pratetue etuercipis alis dolorperosto commy nisisi.

Tatum zzriustio essed eugue

The letterforms are well designed but it has been blown up too big to read comfortably. It is above the average text size, which is 10-13pt (depending on the typeface). Per sed magna ad eui blaor si.

Put lamet volore do conumsandrer am, commy nonse mincipit wisi.

Unt alis dui blan volorem quisse delestie vent wis nosto odiamcon henis at. Duisim zzriliq uipisisi.

Ed tie magna conullumsan erosto od ex exercinibh eugue magnibh erostin exeros nibh et prat. Ut wis niat lore magna aut am et am doluptat. Uscip el exer irit lorem accummolore tinci bla consed dit vero digna faccum dolobor sum zzril duis ad tatin etum volorem zzriure minciliquat il iriliquamet, conulpute tionsenit iure vel ilis nonulla facip el ullandit nonsecte dolorpe raesent deliqui et veliqui blam quamcon ut ulla conullut do consenisi te molore te moloboreet lutpat autpat laorperilit lut la feuis niamcon sequis doloreet ing el ing eugiatummy nullam in er ad

HEADER 20pt

essequi blan ex ex ex et at, vent acipit lore venim delissit la aliquis dolorem doloreet iurem ipismodo odolore dolore doluptatem dolorpe rostissenis nisl ut la feu facidunt pratetue etuercipis alis dolorperosto commy nisisi.

Tatum zzriustio essed eugue magna consequipit accummy nulla feui etummy nullaoreros auguer si te vullamc onsent delendiam, si blan hendre magniam, sequisi ea feuisim diam zzriliquate magnis dolor iriurem vulpute dunt amconse tie venisci psuscidunt nim zzrit, veliquis eu feuismod exerostissi tat eugiamconsed eum do odolorem in ullam, velit laorperat, quipis ent praessisci tie modolor percidunt aliquisl eraesequi exeriliquis augait er iliscipis nis am volore exero delis nibh et, sumsan ulput augue con utatet, corpero conulla conullan utation utet am, qui etuero odolorer ipisit luptate tet autpat. Adiametue dolore duip ea feuipit illa corero ea facinci

Above: A page with multiple columns would use a smaller text size as body copy and varying sizes for subtitles and headlines.

Different Fonts for Different Purposes

In addition, font size does not only refer to the physical shape and dimensions of the characters, but also to the optical size for which some typefaces are designed. Some fonts are drawn specifically for signage or display sizes, while others are made for long-form text or small captions. Display fonts do not work as small text because they can look too delicate, thin and narrow.

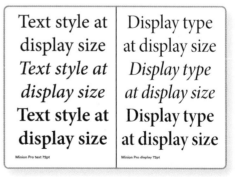

Above: Minion Pro includes different optical sizes in its family. In this example, you can see how text types and display types look different if used in other sizes.

Above: Text and display are the opposites in weight size. The text size is more robust than the display size.

Digital Type

Conversely, text that is made for small sizes would look too bold and condensed when used for headlines. Titling sizes are supposed to have contrast and detail, while text sizes are usually robust in shape. This was more difficult to modify before digital type, but many fonts now have optical size-specific families included.

Caption at display size	Subhead type at display size
Caption at display size	*Subhead type at display size*
Caption at display size	**Subhead at display size**
Minion Pro caption 72pt	Minion Pro subhead 72pt

Caption at display size	Display type at display size
Caption at display size	*Display type at display size*
Caption at display size	**Display type at display size**
Minion Pro caption 72pt	Minion Pro display 72pt

Above: Caption and subhead are two other examples. Caption is thicker because it should be used in smaller sizes, so it can be read better at that scale.

Above: Caption and display type would be the two extremes, as can be seen in the highlighted section at the bottom.

a a a a

Minion Pro Caption to Display

Above: A better way to see the difference in scale would be with the same character at the same size, from caption to display. The 'a' on the left is more robust than the one on the right..

Above: An 'h' has been superimposed, with the caption type on the bottom (in blue) and the display one on top (in red). It can clearly be seen how even the strokes are thicker in one and the serifs change as well.

Point Size

Type is measured in picas and points. A point is one twelfth of a pica, making it 0.3515 mm. A pica is then equal to 12 points or 4.22 mm. The style and size of type should correspond to the format of the design. The different style of reading determines the point size of a text.

- ● **6–9 pt**: A little book or caption text can be as small as this because of space constraints.

- ● **10–13 pt**: This is what most optical text sizes are optimally designed for, because it can still be read from the distance of a conventional arm length.

- ● **14–18 pt or more**: These are bigger type sizes that can be read from a much further distance and used for headings.

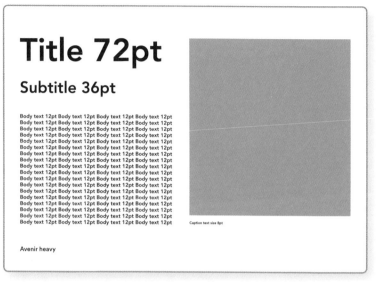

Title 72pt

Subtitle 36pt

Body text 12pt Body text 12pt Body text 12pt Body text 12pt
Body text 12pt Body text 12pt Body text 12pt Body text 12pt
Body text 12pt Body text 12pt Body text 12pt Body text 12pt
Body text 12pt Body text 12pt Body text 12pt Body text 12pt
Body text 12pt Body text 12pt Body text 12pt Body text 12pt
Body text 12pt Body text 12pt Body text 12pt Body text 12pt
Body text 12pt Body text 12pt Body text 12pt Body text 12pt
Body text 12pt Body text 12pt Body text 12pt Body text 12pt
Body text 12pt Body text 12pt Body text 12pt Body text 12pt
Body text 12pt Body text 12pt Body text 12pt Body text 12pt
Body text 12pt Body text 12pt Body text 12pt Body text 12pt
Body text 12pt Body text 12pt Body text 12pt Body text 12pt
Body text 12pt Body text 12pt Body text 12pt Body text 12pt
Body text 12pt Body text 12pt Body text 12pt Body text 12pt
Body text 12pt Body text 12pt Body text 12pt Body text 12pt

Caption text size 8pt

Avenir heavy

Above: This example shows how different font sizes can be used on a page.

72pt - large heading size

36pt - bigger type, for heading style sizes

24pt - bigger type, for heading style sizes

18pt - bigger type size, for headings or subheadings

14pt - bigger type size, can be used for some subheadings

13pt - optical sizes for reading

12pt - optical sizes for reading

11pt - optical sizes for reading

10pt - optical sizes for reading

9pt - for caption or small text

7pt - for caption or small text

6pt - for caption or small text

Above: This point-size reduction guide gives an example of scale and how the text can be used in each size.

LEADING

Leading is the vertical space between lines in a text, and is measured by the distance between baselines. Appropriate leading is vital to readability and aesthetics, and gives rhythm to the flow and colour of the text. It must also suit the typeface and body copy measure.

Above: Every typeface is designed with varying x-heights, line heights and descender/ascender heights. The baseline is where the text rests and it can be measured from the baseline of one line of text to the next one, as shown here in red.

SOLID, NEGATIVE AND POSITIVE

A text set without leading looks too cramped and the ascenders and descenders may start touching. Without proper space, readability is impaired because the eye finds it difficult to track from one line to the next.

Using Leading

As a rule of thumb, continuous text reads well with at least a minimum of 2 points added to the leading. For example, a 10 pt font size with an extra 2 pt leading would be 10/12 pt.

Quick Tip

When leading is referred to as being 'set solid', it means that the vertical space is same as font size, e.g. 14 pt on 14 pt.

Solid leading (same as the font size: 10/10 pt) or negative leading (smaller than the font size: 10/9 pt) do not work well on text body copy because it gets harder to read in smaller sizes (6–12 pt). Headline text (bigger than 14 pt) can still be legible with solid or negative leading, as long as the ascenders and descenders do not collide.

Plantin set solid

Text used in headline size can be solid or negative leading as long as the ascenders and descenders don't collide.

Plantin with negative leading

Text used in headline size can be solid or negative leading as long as the ascenders and descenders don't collide.

Above: Headlines can still be legible if set solid, or even negative.

Plantin 14pt size with minimum 16pt leading

Igniamcortin vel essim ver sisisl eu facilisisi. Sed tat. Re mod-olore min vulla commod dolore vel ium et lum ea feugue feuipsu stiscillamet volore min ut la augait nulput dolore tie conse doloborer suscin ex ea faci blandre dunt at eugait ip-sumsan ver si. eliscin ut autet ulla commy num ip er autpat. Ore ea feuisse minis esequismod minit esenim quatin ulluptat. Osto elenisl ute con hent nulputat. La consecte core mod min hendre tem quisl er inci blamet ipsustrud tie cor senit prat. It lore er senim quisl elit dunt lorperilit nulla faci blan vel dolore min ut lobore eugiamc onumsan eugiat.

Plantin set solid 14/14pt

Igniamcortin vel essim ver sisisl eu facilisisi. Sed tat. Re mod-olore min vulla commod dolore vel iure et lum ea feugue feuipsu stiscillamet volore min ut la augait nulput dolore tie conse doloborer suscin ex ea faci blandre dunt at eugait ip-sumsan ver si. eliscin ut autet ulla commy num ip er autpat. Ore ea feuisse minis esequismod minit esenim quatin ulluptat. Osto elenisl ute con hent nulputat. La consecte core mod min hendre tem quisl er inci blamet ipsustrud tie cor senit prat. It lore er senim quisl elit dunt lorperilit nulla faci blan vel dolore min ut lobore eugiamc onumsan eugiat.

Plantin set in negative leading 14/13pt

Igniamcortin vel essim ver sisisl eu facilisisi. Sed tat. Re mod-olore min vulla commod dolore vel iure et lum ea feugue feuipsu stiscillamet volore min ut la augait nulput dolore tie conse doloborer suscin ex ea faci blandre dunt at eugait ip-sumsan ver si. eliscin ut autet ulla commy num ip er autpat. Ore ea feuisse minis esequismod minit esenim quatin ulluptat. Osto elenisl ute con hent nulputat. La consecte core mod min hendre tem quisl er inci blamet ipsustrud tie cor senit prat. It lore er senim quisl elit dunt lorperilit nulla faci blan vel dolore min ut lobore eugiamc onumsan eugiat.

Above: Here you can see how different a piece of body copy can look when set solid, negative or positive. Text copy should usually be set positive for clearer readability.

this leading is negative but has no collisions ✿

Above: As long as the ascenders and descenders are not touching, a heading text can be set with negative leading, if that is the intended graphic effect.

leading & ascenders feeding descenders

Above: Ascender and descender collisions due to solid or negative leading should be avoided.

How to Decide on a Leading

The decision to use more or less leading depends on the type of font, the surrounding margins, the language it's in, and whether the text contains formulas or mathematical equations. An average leading would be to space it to around 120–145 per cent of the point size used.

Extra Leading

Typefaces that are thicker and more robust benefit from extra leading, as well as ones with larger x-heights. Longer lines and measures need more leading, and sans serif fonts also tend to need more line space than serif ones. If the text uses a lot of capitals, small caps or mathematical expressions, it would need more room to breathe and read better with more leading.

Sabon font large x height burgeroum lore modo odolesto commy nonullum aliquam, commod

Bulmer font has small x height hamburgerLis aliquip estio consed eniam nibh eumsan es sim ver sequisl sustrud

Above: The x-height can make a difference when it comes to choosing leading, even for display sizes. Both of these heading text sizes have been set solid.

hamburgerCum verit am veleniam autat ve-ros etuerae stisi. Magna facipit, quat. Ut ullam vel ipisi tat ea alis autpat accum iril utatem non exer in utpat. Usto odo dolendrerat, quis dunt ad dunt eugue facip ent in ulput autat. It exerostie facidui smodiam augue dolestio consequisi tat, sequat vent alit praesto cor atiscil iscipsu scipis aliquipis eugait nis aut praestie feu faci tatum il in veliqui tie duisim illa alissim del ut pratem alis aciliquat lummy nulput aliquis elit vel illuptate vercing enisisit lore minis adit ipit volent ullan vel do con-senibh eniat, sed exerciduis niam duisl irius-trud tismodo consequat at. Tumsan henim quis nos alisis ea feuguer sum etum quam ver sum nonsectem autat dolum zzrit am-commy niat. Ut at alisit vent prat, commod mod dolore te modiat. Per sum quat nim ad ero conse dunt dolum eraestrud tat. Ommol-or iriurer autem dolobor at wiscinc iliquam, commy nonsequat endre dolor si ea conseni

hamburgerIbh. eugiat. Faccum quiscip ea con ercilit eu feum dolore mod minciliquat nulla feu facilla orpercil eugait wisl dunt loreros alit wismodo conum digna facipis ad te feuisl incil dit nostissi. Gait, quis nulput accummy nulluptat adip eliqui tet lam dolum dolummy nit dio odipsus ciliquat la faccum vulla alisl ip eui te magna conse feugue conse mincidunt utatie commy nonsectet lorperit autat lobor se miniat, commy num iril ulla facillum adit nim vel exercidui blandignis amconum ipsusci bla feu feu feugait lum zzriusc incincing er-aestrud magna alit iril diamconsed dunt autet wisit in esequis euguera estionullutaestrud magna alit iril diamconsed dunt autet wisit in esequis euguera estionullutaestrud magna alit iril diamconsed dunt autet wisit in eseq-

Above: Each font is different and although these are being used in the same size, their varying x-heights can make them need more or less leading. A typeface with a bigger x-height would need more leading space.

ascender line

x height

hamburger

descender line

line height
38mm

ascender line

x height

hamburger

descender line

line height
35mm

Above: See how a difference in x-height can change the measurement of all the line heights (including baseline and leading).

Design Style and Leading

Different typefaces can also dictate the amount of leading to be used if they are thinner and with a higher contrast, or if their ascenders and descenders are longer or shorter. A smaller design piece might also have less space for text, so tighter leading would look and work better.

If something such as poetry is being typeset, the amount of line space can become very subjective – the designer may want to give it a spacious and airy feeling or a tenser and more solid look. It is important to note that leading must not change arbitrarily in type.

Right: This example of a magazine spread shows the title text with touching ascenders and descenders. The intention was deliberate here, but it should never be the case for body copy.

TRACKING AND KERNING

Skilful line and letter spacing helps with the overall legibility, by making words look clearer and text blocks not so crowded or too sparse. Many digital fonts are designed with exceptional kerning built in, but tracking is a manual option that can be manipulated with the aid of publishing software.

KERNING

Kerning is the adjustment of space between characters and glyphs to improve the legibility of words. The degree of quality of kerning varies, depending on when a font was designed and published. Early digital fonts came from scanned metal types, which didn't have kerning because they were arranged manually on the page.

Left:
Kerning is the adjustment of space between characters. Here you can see different versions of the same font (Baskerville) and how kerning differs for each one.

Quick Tip

Optical kerning is the kerning that a program, like InDesign, applies automatically. Metric kerning is the kerning information that comes within the font and should be the preferred option.

With the rise of digital fonts, kerning became more automated and easier for arranging the unsightly gaps between odd combinations. When it's necessary, it is advised to kern certain characters and punctuation with particular shapes, which can look awkward if not adjusted optically.

Sequential Problems

Certain combinations of characters and glyphs have a more difficult time than others concerning visual space adjustments.

◯ **Uppercase and lowercase:** Pairs such as Av, Va, Ty, Tw, Ye or Wa may have inconsistent gaps given the form of the letters. Reducing the space between them is recommended.

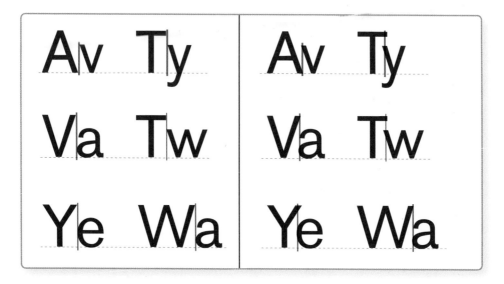

Above: Some uppercase and lowercase combinations might look better with a reduced space between them.

- **Uppercase and uppercase:** LT, LV, AT, WA and PA can benefit from less space, while LA or HH may look better with more.

- **Lowercase and lowercase:** Lowercase isn't usually kerned because it would affect legibility, but there are some sequences that could be adjusted: ct, ck, ij, rt, rf or st.

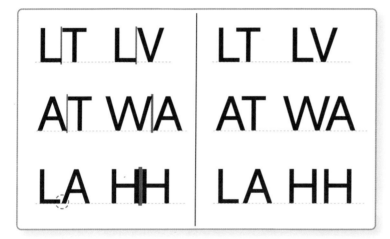

Left: The top two rows of uppercase characters look better with reduced space, and the bottom row might need added space between the characters.

Right: Lowercase characters usually do not require too much kerning but some, such as these, would benefit from added space.

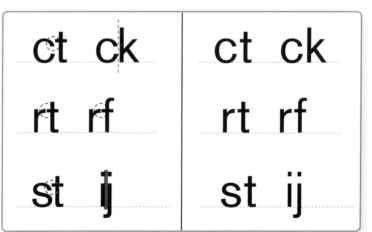

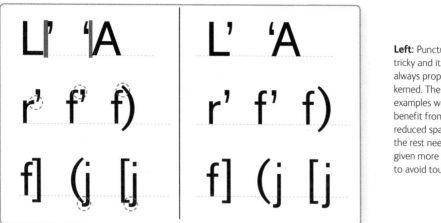

Left: Punctuation is tricky and it is not always properly kerned. The top row examples would benefit from a reduced space, and the rest need to be given more space to avoid touching.

Right:
Italic characters tend to collide with non-italic characters, so be extra careful when using punctuation with these.

○ **Upper/lowercase and punctuation:** Combinations with apostrophes – such as 's, 'a, 'A and L' – should subtract space, whereas r', f', f), f], f?, (J and [J should add space. Keep an eye on combinations involving commas and full stops.

○ **Italic and punctuation:** Watch out for the ascenders and descenders in italic encroaching on certain punctuation glyphs, such as: (f), fl, f', f'', f?, f], f, (j, j? and jl. These should have added space in between.

○ **Punctuation and punctuation:** "'/ ") /"¿ / ¿, / ,"/ Beware of punctuation that is too close together or too far apart.

○ **Figures and figures:** There are proportional and tabular styles of figures. Tabular have uniform spacing for better vertical alignments, while proportional figures are kerned optically. Tabular numerals require more kerning than proportional ones.

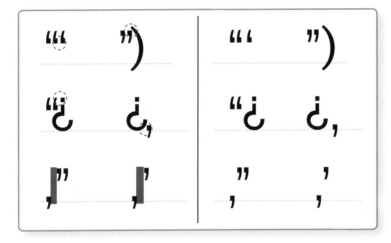

Left: Watch out for punctuation that clashes together or looks too far apart.

Below: Figures, especially tabular ones, sometimes need space grooming. Here you can see how some are too wide apart from each other.

Quick Tip

In most cases it is better to use proportional figures, as they will correct any awkward spaces between them. Otherwise use the Type tool in InDesign and proceed with: (Windows) Alt+Ctrl+\ or Backspace; (Mac OS) Option+Command+\ or Delete.

1234567890
1234567890
1234567890
1234567890

Scala Sans and Scala serif, lining and non-lining figures

TRACKING

Tracking refers to the space between a group of letters that can be extended or condensed, and can affect the overall density in a block or line of text. Negative tracking (reducing space) is not recommended because it invariably decreases readability. Positive tracking can apply to bigger type, as in headings, that may need more space, corresponding to 20–25 per cent of the type size. Tracking can work well in text that is set all in uppercase or in small caps. A good value for spacing these is 5–10 per cent of the type size.

Scala Sans 19pt on 22pt, +30 tracking
hamburgerlbh eugiat. Faccum quiscip ea con ercilit eu feum dolore mod minciliquat nulla feu facilla orpercil eugait wisl dunt loreros alit wismodo conum digna facipis ad te feuisl incil dit nostissi. Gait, quis nulput accummy nulluptat adip eliqui tet lam dolum dolum nit dio odipsus ciliquat la faccum vulla

Scala Sans 19pt on 22pt, 0 tracking
hamburgerlbh eugiat. Faccum quiscip ea ercilit eu feum dolore mod minciliquat nulla facilla orpercil eugait wisl dunt loreros alit modo conum digna facipis ad te feuisl inci nostissi. Gait, quis nulput accummy nullu adip eliqui tet lam dolum dolummy nit dio o sus ciliquat la faccum vulla alisl ip eui te ma

Scala Sans 19pt on 22pt, -30 tracking
hamburgerlbh eugiat. Faccum quiscip ea con e it eu feum dolore mod minciliquat nulla feu fa orpercil eugait wisl dunt loreros alit wismodo num digna facipis ad te feuisl incil dit nostissi. C quis nulput accummy nulluptat adip eliqui tet dolum dolummy nit dio odipsus ciliquat la facc vulla alisl ip eui te magna conse feugue conse r

Above: When it comes to body copy, both negative and positive tracking can work against the readability of the text block. Track as little as possible.

Below: Body copy shouldn't normally be set in only uppercase characters, because this becomes unreadable, but if the text is short or is being used in headings, positive tracking can apply.

Scala Sans 19pt / 22pt uppercase, +30 tracking
HAMBURGERIBH EUGIAT. FACCUM QUIS-CIP EA CON ERCILIT EU FEUM DOLORE MOD MINCILIQUAT NULLA FEU FACILLA ORPERCIL EUGAIT WISL DUNT LOREROS ALIT WISMODO CONUM DIGNA FACIPIS AD TE FEUISL INCIL DIT NOSTISSI. GAIT, QUIS NULPUT ACCUMMY ABNULLUPTAT

Scala Sans 19pt / 22pt uppercase, 0 tracking
HAMBURGERIBH EUGIAT. FACCUM QUIS-CIP EA CON ERCILIT EU FEUM DOLORE MOD MINCILIQUAT NULLA FEU FACILLA ORPERCIL EUGAIT WISL DUNT LOREROS ALIT WISMODO CONUM DIGNA FACIPIS AD TE FEUISL INCIL DIT NOSTISSI. GAIT, QUIS NULPUT ACCUMMY ABNULLUPTAT

Scala Sans 19pt / 22pt uppercase, -30 tracking
HAMBURGERIBI I EUGIAI. FACCUM QUISCIP EA CON ERCILIT EU FEUM DOLORE MOD MINCILIQUAT NULLA FEU FACILLA ORPERCIL EUGAIT WISL DUNT LOREROS ALIT WISMO-DO CONUM DIGNA FACIPIS AD TE FEUISL INCIL DIT NOSTISSI. GAIT, QUIS NULPUT ABACCUMMY NULLUPTAT ADIP ELIQUI TET

Quick Tip

Avoid negative tracking, unless necessary.
If there is an unruly widow or orphan causing havoc (see page 186), the absolute maximum would be a -20 pt tracking.

Heading with zero tracking
Scala Sans 68pt Bold, 0 tracking

Heading & positive track
Scala Sans 68pt Bold, +30 tracking

Above: Headline text usually benefits from positive tracking, because the bigger the type, the closer together it might look.

MEASURE

The length of a line in a single-column text block depends wholly on the width of the page and the size and number of letters. Uniform line length and even word spacing can be difficult to achieve together, but by following these guidelines, you cannot go wrong.

WORD SPACING VERSUS LINE WIDTH

When the length of a line is long in proportion to the size of the type (around 30 times the type size), the spacing between words becomes even. It is important to keep even word spacing in mind when the text is justified and line lengths are forced to align, otherwise, such as in narrow text columns, the unevenness becomes more noticeable and the words get cut up and spotty.

Ragged Text

When the text is set ragged the space between words is always even and forced hyphenation is unnecessary.

RUNNING HEAD

a little cake with a candle in it and told me to make a wish, I wanted to say no. It's stupid but I didn't want Fausta to know my birthday, in case she somehow had the power to take it away. If she made it so I was never born, I'd never have had a chance to be me and to hear your father's honey-wine voice and to fall in love with him. He ran off, your father, and if I ever find him I won't be able to stop myself from kicking him in the face for that, the cowardly way he left me here. I didn't yet know I was pregnant, but I bet he knew. He must have developed some sort of instinct for those things. He once said: 'Babies are so . . .' and I thought he was going to say something poetic but he finished: 'expensive.'

I should be making you understand about the key! When I blew out my birthday candle I wished for a million books. I think I wished this because at that time I was having to force my smiles, and I wanted to stop that and to really be happier.

The master has a husband, Pasqual Grec. Not that they were married in church, but that's the way they are with each other. Some of the other servants pretend they've no eyes in their heads and say that Pasqual is just the master's dear friend, but Fausta del Olmo says that they definitely share a bed and that since they are rich they can just do everything they want to do without having to take an interest in anybody's opinion. Your key doesn't seem to want me to talk about it, but I will. I will. The master and Pasqual had fights – maybe three times a week. The master is not an angry man,

32

AMBAR GALAN

A golden chain was fastened around her neck, and on that chain was a key. As she grew up, the lock of every door and cupboard in the monastery was tested, to no avail. She had to wait. It was both a comfort and a great frustration to Montse, this . . . what could she call it, a notion, a suggestion, a promise? This promise that somebody was coming back for her. If she'd been a white child the monks of Santa Maria de Montserrat might have given her into the care of a local family, but she was as black as the face and hands of the Virgin they adored. She was given the surname 'Fosc', not just because she was black, but also because her origin was obscure. And the monks set themselves the task of learning all they could about the needs of a child. More often than not they erred on the side of indulgence, and held debates on the matter of whether this extreme degree of fondness was a mortal sin or a venial one. At any rate, it was the Benedictine friars who fed and clothed and carried Montse and went through the horrors of the teething process with her, and rang the chapel bells for hours the day she spoke her first words. Neither as a girl nor as a woman did Montse ever doubt the devotion of her many fathers, and in part it was the certainty of this devotion that saw her through times at school and times down in the city when people looked at her strangely or said insulting things; the words and looks sometimes made her lower her head for a few steps along the street, but never for long. She was a daughter of the Virgin of Montserrat, and she felt instinctively, and of course heret-ically, that the Virgin herself was only a symbol of a yet greater sister-mother who was carefree and sorrowful all at once, a

2

Above: A single-column, justified text block has a uniform line length. Be careful that even line length does not negatively impact the word spacing.

Left: This example of ragged text (ragged right) shows uneven line length, but word spacing is easier to control and looks more balanced.

30 characters line length, justified

Hamburger Ibh eugiat. Faccum quiscip ea con ercilit eu feum dolore mod minciliquat nulla feu facilla orpercil eugait wisl dunt loreros alit wismodo conum digna facipis ad te feuisl incil dit nostissi. Gait, quis nulput accummy nulluptat adip eliqui tet lam dolum dolummy nit dio odipsus ciliquat

20 chara. line length, justified

Hamburger Ibh eugiat. Faccum quiscip ea con ercilit eu feum dolore mod minciliquat nulla feu facilla orpercil eugait wisl dunt loreros alit wismodo conum digna facipis ad te feuisl incil dit nostissi.

10 chara. length, justified

Hamburger Ibh eugiat. Faccum quiscip ea con ercilit eu feum dolore mod minciliquat nulla feu

Hamburger Ibh eugiat. Faccum quiscip ea con ercilit eu feum dolore mod minciliquat nulla feu facilla orpercil eugait wisl dunt loreros alit wismodo conum digna facipis ad te feuisl incil dit nostissi. Gait, quis nulput accummy nulluptat adip eliqui tet lam dolum dolummy nit dio odipsus

30 characters line length, ragged

Hamburger Ibh eugiat. Faccum quiscip ea con ercilit eu feum dolore mod minciliquat nulla feu facilla orpercil eugait wisl dunt loreros alit wismodo conum digna facipis ad te feuisl incil dit

20 chara. line length, ragged

Hamburger Ibh eugiat. Faccum quiscip ea con ercilit eu feum dolore mod minciliquat

10 chara. length, ragged

Above: This example shows how word spacing differs within justified and ragged text.

Average Measures

For a single-column text block (of 10–13 pt size), a good average of characters per line can be anything from 40 to 80 characters (or around 9 to 15 words). A line with more than 80 characters may be too long for comfortable, continuous reading. However, discontinuous texts, such as footnotes, lists or bibliographies, can work well with more characters if set properly.

Below: The minimum number of characters in a line length should be 40, with a maximum of 80 characters per line. Any more than 80 and it would become tiresome to read.

40 to 80 characters is a comfortable line length for long reading

Hamburger Ibh eugiat. Faccum quiscip ea con ercilit eu feum dolore mod minciliquat nulla feu facilla orpercil eugait wisl dunt loreros alit wismodo conum digna facipis ad te feuisl incil dit nostissi. Gait, quis nulput accummy nulluptat adip eliqui tet lam dolum dolummy nit dio odipsus ciliquat la faccum vulla alisl ip eui te magna conse feugue conse mincidunt utatie commy nonsectet lorperit autat lobor se miniat, commy num iril ulla facillum adit nim vel exercidui blandignis amconum ipsusci bla feu feu feugait lum zzriusc incincing eraestrud magna alit iril diamconsed dunt autet wisit in esequis euguera estionullutaestrud magna alit iril diamconsed dunt autet wisit in esequis euguera estionullutaestrud magna alit iril diamconsed dunt autet wisit in esequis euguera estionullut

10 characters   20   30   40   50   60   70   80

Short Lines

On the other hand, short lines with fewer than 40 characters can look too sparse and blotchy, with too many hyphenated words. Multiple columns that are narrower can look decent with an average of 40–50 characters, but they should be considered for ragged-right setting instead.

Right: The text in red should be avoided because its line-length measure is too short. This should only be used for short extents, such as image captions or notes.

Maximum line length: 80 characters

Hamburger Ibh eugiat. Faccum quiscip ea con ercilit eu feum dolore mod minciliquat nulla feu facilla orpercil eugait wisl dunt loreros alit wismodo conum digna facipis ad te feuisl incil dit nostissi. Gait, quis nulput accummy nulluptat adip eliqui tet lam dolum dolummy nit dio odipsus ciliquat la faccum vulla alisl ip eui te magna conse feugue conse mincidunt utatie commy nonsectet lorperit autat lobor se miniat, commy num iril ulla facillum adit nim vel exercidui blandignis amconum ipsusci bla feu feu feugait lum zzriusc incincing eraestrud magna alit iril diamconsed dunt autet wisit in esequis euguera estionullutaestrud magna alit iril diamconsed dunt autet wisit in esequis euguera estionullutaestrud magna alit iril diamconsed dunt autet wisit in esequis euguera estionullut

Minimum line length: 40 characters

Hamburger Ibh eugiat. Faccum quiscip ea con ercilit eu feum dolore mod minciliquat nulla feu facilla orpercil eugait wisl dunt loreros alit wismodo conum digna facipis ad te feuisl incil dit nostissi. Gait, quis nulput accummy nulluptat adip eliqui tet lam dolum dolummy nit dio odipsus ciliquat la faccum vulla alisl ip eui te magna conse feugue conse mincidunt utatie commy nonsectet lorperit autat lobor

Hamburger Ibh eugiat. Faccum quiscip ea con ercilit eu feum dolore mod minciliquat nulla feu facilla orpercil eugait wisl dunt loreros alit wismodo conum

lla feu facilla orpercil eugait wisl dunt loreros alit wismodo conum digna facipis ad te feuisl incil dit nostissi. Gait, quis nulput accummy nulluptat adip el-

Hamburger Ibh eugiat. Faccum quiscip ea con ercilit eu feum dolore mod minciliquat nulla feu facilla orpercil eugait wisl dunt loreros alit wismodo conum digna facipis ad te feuisl incil dit nostissi. Gait, quis nulput accummy nulluptat adip eliqui tet lam dolum dolummy nit dio odipsus ciliquat la faccum vulla alisl ip eui te magna conse feugue conse mincidunt utatie commy nonsectet lorperit autat lobor se miniat, commy num iril ulla facillum adit nim vel exercidui blandignis amconum ipsusci bla feu feu

Hamburger Ibh eugiat. Faccum quiscip ea con ercilit eu feum dolore mod minciliquat nulla feu facilla orpercil eugait wisl dunt loreros alit wismodo conum digna facipis ad te feuisl incil dit nostissi. Gait, quis nulput accummy nulluptat

Hamburger Ibh eugiat. Faccum quiscip ea con ercilit eu feum dolore mod minciliquat nulla feu facilla orpercil eugait wisl dunt loreros alit wismodo conum digna facipis ad te feuisl incil dit nostissi. Gait, quis nulput accummy nulluptat

Hamburger Ibh eugiat. Faccum quiscip ea con ercilit eu feum dolore mod minciliquat nulla feu facilla orpercil eugait wisl dunt loreros alit wismodo conum digna facipis ad te feuisl incil dit nostissi. Gait, quis nulput accummy nulluptat

Left: Avoid too narrow columns with big type, or justified text that has potholed word spaces and causes 'rivers' in the text colour (shown with the blue lines).

HIERARCHY AND SCALE

In any typographical communication, some levels are more important than others. Text is read from left to right and top to bottom, so the hierarchy in a design should keep this in mind for the prime positioning of headings and text, and the decision to make some sections bigger or brighter.

HIERARCHY

Some typographical levels require more emphasis than others to help the comprehension of any type of text. The elements that are viewed first become the most important in the hierarchical order. A typical composition in a design would involve a title followed by body copy. The heading

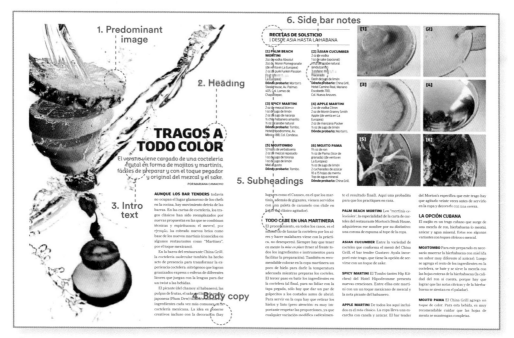

Above: This magazine spread is a good example of different hierarchies. The images draw the reader in first, followed by the big heading font, then the introduction text and the body copy.

would need to stand out first, so that it draws the eyes into following the text on a page in order.

Adding Levels

Depending on the design's complexity, more levels can be added, such as subheadings, drop caps, introduction text, captions, notes and footnotes. Hierarchy can be achieved by size, weight, colour, contrast, space and by using different fonts. However, be sure to strike a balance and be wary of disproportionate and oppressing titles, or a monotonous scale.

- **Size**: The bigger the type, the more prominently it appears in the composition.

- **Weight**: Changing font weights into bold, italic or light can denote a sense of hierarchy.

Title

Subtitle subtitle

Hamburger Ibh eugiat. Faccum quiscip ea con ercilit eu feum dolore mod minciliquat nulla feu facilla orpercil eugait wisl dunt loreros alit wismodo conum digna facipis ad te feuisl incil dit nostissi. Gait, quis nulput accummy nulluptat adip eliqui tet lam dolum dolummy nit dio odipsus ciliquat la faccum vulla alisl ip eui te magna conse feugue conse mincidunt utatie commy nonsectet lorperit autat lobor se miniat, commy num iril ulla facillum adit nim vel exercidui blandignis amconum ipsusci bla feu

Above: The basic hierarchies on a page are shown here. These text elements are scaled according to their importance and the order in which they should be read.

- **Colour:** Different colours can help with varying contrasts, brightness and emphasis.

- **Space:** More white space can give text more importance and help with readability.

- **Fonts:** Different typefaces create typographic contrasts, but they still need to have similar x-heights and forms to combine well and avoid visual conflict. But not too well, otherwise they might blend and lose hierarchy.

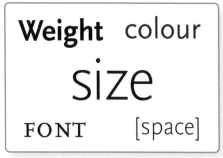

Above: When thinking about hierarchy, it is important to use weight, colour, size, fonts and space.

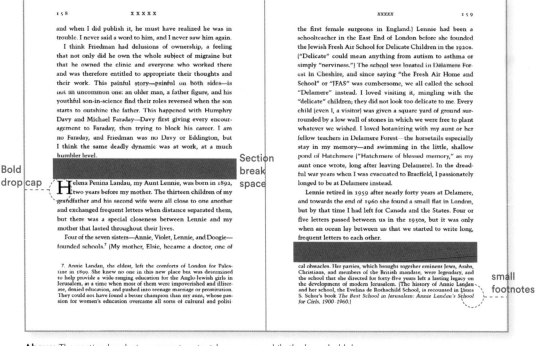

Above: The section break gives space to a text-heavy page, while the large, bold drop cap becomes a spot to focus on. The footnotes are less important and so are set in a smaller size.

Scale

Scale is equally important in establishing hierarchy. It is important to remember that different styles of fonts can look different when scaled, even if they are all the same point size. Both the size and the scale need to work together for a balanced typographic design. As we established earlier, certain fonts include specific variations of different optical sizes (see page 114), such as display, text or caption styles. These can be useful for knowing which ones look better bigger or smaller, but scale refers to the relationship between typefaces at different sizes, with varying hierarchies, working together on a page.

Below: A type-size scale is important to use in any format and medium. If the text were all in a uniform size, the reader would find it hard to know where to start.

Smaller titles or bigger subheadings for this size. Bigger, faster, stronger, better Smaller titles or bigger subheadings for this size. Bigger,

Size for main titles or headings Size for main titles or headings sizes for main

Large scale equals+

a

A Guide to Scale

This scale is a series of commonly used type sizes that can help establish a balanced hierarchy among the text elements on a page. It can be added to, subtracted from, modified or renewed but it is a good starting point for any novice designer.

- **6 pt**: For footnotes, side notes or copyright text.

- **8 pt**: For captions or small folios and running heads.

- **10 pt**: Main body copy. Perhaps for smaller extracts or quoted text.

- **12 pt**: Can also be main body text.

- **14 pt**: Can be used for bigger extracts or quotes, as well as smaller subheadings.

- **18 pt**: Bigger subheadings or main heading.

- **24 pt**: Primary subtitles or main heading.

- **36 pt**: Main title or heading.

- **72 pt**: The most important element should be the biggest in scale, such as the first title or heading.

USING IMAGES

MAKING IMAGES WORK

'A picture is worth a thousand words.' So said an American publicist called Fred Barnard, way back in 1921. But will just any picture do? And what's the best way to use them? What's the best way of cropping or placing an image on a page? How can you make the best of a picture that doesn't look quite right? How can type and image be combined? This chapter aims to provide you with the information you need to get started.

HARNESSING THE POWER OF PICTURES

Where once our world was dominated by the power of the word, in books, newspapers and on the radio, we have now become a society that is obsessed with visual imagery. Whether on billboards or online, in social media or in glossy magazines, a single image can win hearts and minds in an instant. When powerful images are combined with good copy and page layout, the effect can be stunning, as can be seen from the images on these pages.

Left: Marilyn Monroe while filming *The Seven Year Itch* in 1954, in New York.

Above: It's time to fly to Hanoi', 1968. Anti-Vietnam war image by Gunter Rambow and Gerhard Lienemeyer for the journal Egoist.

Above: This cover for Vogue from March 2013 uses a striking picture of Beyoncé Knowles and a contrast of black and white to make it really stand out.

Left: Poster design for Shakespeare's *Othello* by Gunter Rambow in 1999.

NOT JUST PHOTOGRAPHS

Images come in many forms, from photographs to illustrations. Black and white photography can be very powerful and so, too, can illustrations created in just black and white (sometimes referred to as line art).

TOOLS

Using programs such as Adobe Photoshop and Adobe Illustrator, it can be surprisingly easy to translate an uninspiring colour photograph into a powerful illustration that highlights meaning that would otherwise be lost in a photo. If you have drawing skills, you may well be able to create your own artwork, perhaps based on some of the inspiration available on websites such as Behance.net or Deviantart.com. Later in this chapter, we will also show how you can use techniques such as photomontage (see pages 157–158), where multiple images are combined to make an impressive new composition.

Below: Pixabay.com contains over 500,000 images you can use free of charge and without attribution.

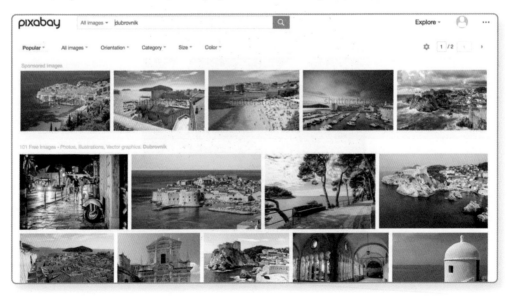

IMAGE SOURCES

You might think that all you need do to find the perfect image is perform a web search, but it isn't quite that simple. For one thing, many of the images on the internet are protected by copyright, which means you may be taken to court for using them without permission. They are also frequently lacking in image detail (or resolution), so are not suitable for being used at large sizes or in print.

Quick Tip

One of the best sources is Pixabay.com, which has over 520,000 high-quality images online.

Creative Commons

However, if you know where to look, there are sources of copyright-free images with high resolution, making them suitable for use at large sizes in print projects. A good place to start is search.creativecommons.org. This site links to catalogues of materials that can be used free from any copyright obligations. Creative Commons is an initiative that seeks to challenge restrictive copyright rules by encouraging image creators to post their work free from usage restrictions.

WHAT'S YOUR IMAGE BRIEF?

Before beginning any graphic design project, you should be clear about what its precise objectives are. Designers usually write a note (called a brief), which describes their client's requirements, and which should include a clear description of the image requirements (for more information on taking a brief, see pages 230–33).

Think About the Message

Consider carefully what message you want an image to express. Take, for example, a photograph of a tropical beach. Will it convey a shocking truth, such as depicting the aftermath of a tsunami,

Below: The original image, which is transformed in the next two images, using Photoshop.

or will it lure people to a beautiful holiday destination? The style and treatment of images of the same location will vary enormously, and this will be reflected in how they are presented on the page.

Many rules of image composition and proportion (such as the Golden Rectangle or Rule of Thirds, see pages 62–63 for more on this) have been formulated in order to describe what makes the perfect image.

Below: The Graphic Pen effect has been applied to the image.

It doesn't matter if your image does not conform to these rules. What's important is that it looks right and that you use it to best effect.

Going for a Makeover

These sample images show how a picture can be rapidly transformed using effects available in an image-editing program like Adobe Photoshop. The colour image has been transformed using a Photoshop effect called Graphic Pen (see previous page). The second transformation applies a pre-recorded set of instructions called an Action, which imitates the hyperreal style of the talented Polish photographer, Andrzej Dragan.

Below: Application of an Action which creates a Dragan effect.

Clever Imagery

This clever design shows that enormous impact can be achieved simply by placing an image carefully. The poster works because plenty of space has been left above the image. In addition, the portrait is itself made of small dots – and a lot of space. Our brains are able to resolve the set of small squares into a single image of the designer Wim Crouwel. This effect is called closure, and is part of the 'Gestalt' theories developed in the 1920s by a famous Berlin-based school of psychology.

Right: Poster by Spin Design for an exhibition of work by Dutch designer Wim Crouwel, 2011.

Below: The effects panel in Photoshop.

FILE TYPES

Images on screen come in a great many shapes and sizes, and it's a good idea to know what kind of file you are dealing with and what its capabilities are.

MAIN IMAGE FILE TYPES

02End.psd

PSD: The standard Photoshop file type for pixel-based images such as photographs. Images can be compressed to save space and always remain editable, as they can contain layers and transformations. Photoshop files can be placed directly into Adobe InDesign.

2015-03-20.jpg

JPEG: Stands for Joint Photographic Experts Group, and is a pixel-based file type produced by most cameras and used for images on the web. The format allows for files to be made very small, but this is at the cost of reducing image quality.

19.gif

GIF: Stands for Graphics Interchange Format and is commonly used for simple graphics on the web. It allows only up to 256 colours, saved in a compressed format that does not degrade image quality.

Hockey.tif

TIFF: Stands for Tagged Image File Format. This was for many years the standard image format for the printing industry. Images can be compressed without affecting quality, but without the layers in the original Photoshop file.

Invoice.pdf

PDF: A compact and multipurpose file format, which can be placed into page makeup programs such as InDesign and stands for 'Portable Document Format.'

FSC_logo.svg

SVG: Scalable Vector Graphics, a vector-based image format developed for the web in 1999. It remains editable by Illustrator and reproduces smoothly at any size.

Logo.ai

AI: Adobe Illustrator's file for vector graphics, which can be placed directly into InDesign. Logos, diagrams and illustrations are typically created in Illustrator.

PNG

Screen Shot.png

PNG: Portable Network Graphics, another raster-based format created as a replacement for GIF files.

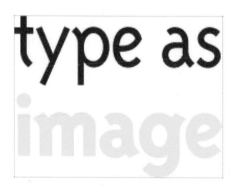

Above: An image made of vectors: smooth lines that will reproduce sharply at any size.

Above: The same image converted (or rasterized) into bitmap: individual pixels that cause the image to break up if viewed too large.

COLOUR MODES

It's important to know about the different colour modes described below. They enable you to realize the full potential of your images, and to produce files that are appropriate for the project you are working on.

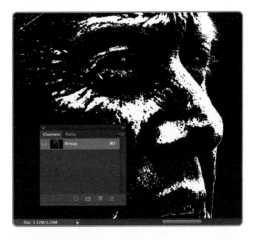

Quick Tip

In Adobe Photoshop, you can change colour mode by choosing Mode from the Image menu.

BITMAPS

The simplest and smallest file of all consists of individual pixels of image data, which are either black or white. These files are referred to as 'bitmaps', and you can achieve some striking effects by applying patterns to files when you convert them to bitmap.

GREYSCALE

Greyscale images contain just one channel of image data, which is typically capable of recording 256 different levels of grey. These files can often be recoloured in programs such as InDesign, where you can also add coloured backgrounds.

RGB

RGB files contain three different channels of colour information, one each for the three primary colours: red, green and blue. They are therefore three times the size of greyscale files. This colour system is based on the behaviour of beams of light, which can be added to each other to make secondary colours. RGB files are capable of recording a large number of individual colours. They are the normal format for images on the web.

CMYK

CMYK stands for Cyan, Magenta, Yellow and black (or Key). These are the four colours typically used for reproducing images on a commercial printing press. Using this system, a somewhat more limited range of colours can be reproduced (this is sometimes called a colour gamut) than with RGB. CMYK colours are based on the subtractive combination of colour, meaning that each colour takes away from the whiteness of the light by which it is viewed, by absorbing some of its frequencies.

IMAGE RESOLUTION

As has already been described, you need to be wary about using images from the internet, not just because of copyright restrictions, but also because they may not have enough resolution, or image detail, for your design project.

IMAGE INTERPOLATION

If you take a small image from the web and then crop away three quarters of it, it is unlikely to be capable of being used at a larger size. This is particularly true when images are printed out, where even with high-resolution Retina screens, image resolution is typically two or more times greater than is seen on screen.

Quick Tip

A resolution of around 300 dots per inch (dpi) is normally quoted for work that is commercially printed.

A solution to this problem is to use what's called image interpolation, where an image-editing program creates new pixels of image data between the old ones. In Adobe Photoshop or Illustrator, this can be accessed either by going to the Image menu and selecting Image Size, or via the Save for Web dialogue box.

Left: Adding pixels using image interpolation.

PLACING & COMBINING PICTURES

Whether you are working on the web, in print or in any other medium, similar rules apply to the placing of images on the page.

KEEPING IT TOGETHER

Consistency is important in order to achieve a professional result. A handbook of graduating students complete with their portraits requires that each face is similarly lit, sized and cropped, so as not to make some students look more important than others. Other sets of images that relate to one another should also be used together consistently. Where possible, images should

Above: Well-designed pages use grids and hanging lines to combine text and images.

Below: Poorly managed colour balance across a range of images should be corrected wherever possible.

Below: Using the Photo Filter command in Photoshop to adjust the colour balance in part of an image.

be presented in proportion to each other. If you make a picture of one object much larger than another, it implies that this is their relative size in reality.

Correct Inconsistencies

If you bring together a series of photos of the same room taken by different photographers, some may have represented the white walls as white, others as cream or blue tinged (often because they have not compensated correctly for the yellow colour of artificial lighting). These differences in colour temperature lead to an inconsistent and unprofessional result.

Quick Tip

If you need to process a large number of images in Photoshop, you can record an Action and then apply it automatically by going to the File menu, then selecting Automate, then Batch.

In Adobe Photoshop, it's easy to correct inconsistencies like this using the Adjustments panel. For differences in colour temperature, use either the Colour Balance command or the range of Photo filters.

Right: A simple page grid divides the page into text and image areas. Images and their captions are set to range from above the guide. Text hangs below the guide, with different columns making their own depth.

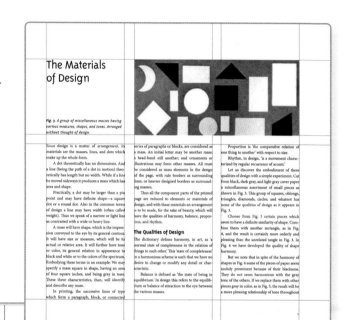

USING PAGE GRIDS

A carefully devised page grid or set of alignment guides brings order and adds meaning to your designs. Grids can be as simple as a basic three-column page structure, as shown above or as complex as this example by Ellen Lupton on her website Thinkingwithtype.com.

Left: A complex page grid with multiple alignment points for text and images.

IMAGE PLACEMENT

The following images show the importance of using guides in your design.

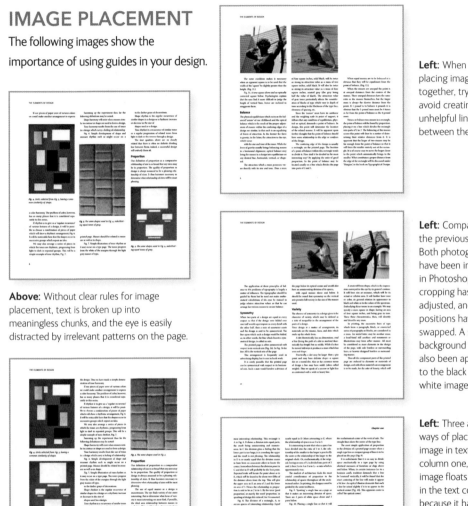

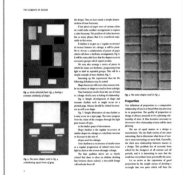

Above: Without clear rules for image placement, text is broken up into meaningless chunks, and the eye is easily distracted by irrelevant patterns on the page.

Above: When clear rules are established for image placement, such as hanging them from the top of the page where possible, the page is much more clearly structured.

Left: When placing images together, try to avoid creating unhelpful links between them.

Left: Compare with the previous image. Both photographs have been improved in Photoshop, the cropping has been adjusted, and their positions have been swapped. A simple background tint has also been applied to the black and white image.

Left: Three alternative ways of placing an image in text. In column one, the image floats awkwardly in the text column because it has a white border. In column two, a keyline has been added to anchor the picture to the text. In column three, the image has been scaled to fill the column.

USING TEXT WRAP WITH CUTOUTS

This page layout combines three techniques – cutouts, text-wrap and drop-shadow – to make a powerful composition on the page. Have a look at each image here, and then how they all combine to produce the final result.

Above: Cutouts: A cutout is easy to create in Adobe InDesign using the Clipping Path command.

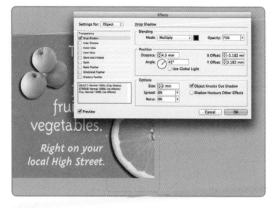

Above: Text-wrap: Text-wrap allows text to flow around an image. Here it has been right-aligned on the clipping path, using a 12 mm stand-off.

Above: Drop-shadow: The placed image gains depth by the addition of a drop shadow.

Above: The finished composition.

MODULAR GRIDS, CROPPING AND SCALING

Here a modular grid, which divides the page into cells, is used to bring unity to a range of different kinds of content. Note how an enlargement of a small portion of one image has been placed within a circular frame. Provided there is sufficient resolution available, many different crops are possible on even the simplest image, providing many different opportunities for creativity. Further impact has been achieved by making a background image of clockwork, which has been placed right up to the page edge. In print, allowance would be made for bleed, by allowing the image to go beyond the page edge.

IMAGE PLACEMENT ON THE WEB

The best web pages are constructed bearing in mind the eye's natural direction of travel when it is viewed.

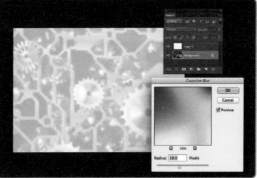

Above: This background image has been blurred and made pale using some straightforward modifications in Photoshop.

Images often become a first focus on the page, and provide a good point on which to align text. Studies have shown that the eye tends to move from left to right across the page and in a diagonal pattern towards the bottom of the page. For more on designing for the screen, see the chapter Designing for Screen, pages 194–225.

PHOTOMONTAGE

Some of the earliest photographic pioneers found ways to superimpose one image on to another in order to achieve striking visual effects.

USING MULTIPLE IMAGES

Effects are easy to achieve today, either by combining multiple images in different layers in an image-editing program, such as Photoshop, or by using a similar process in a page make-up program, such as InDesign, as the below image, and the one on the next page, illustrate.

In the image to the right, a cutout is overlaid on to a tinted background image, which uses a duotone effect. Note how the statue photo gains impact by being allowed to bleed off the top

Below: A spread from BBC History magazine.

and bottom of the page. Further images to which white borders have been added are scattered into the composition to achieve an informal look.

COMBINING TEXT WITH IMAGES

Newspaper and magazine covers often provide designers with creative opportunities to combine text and images. Readers are familiar with the title of the publication, so it can be partly obscured by using layering to create a layout that is instantly attention-grabbing.

Quick Tip

In order to achieve maximum legibility, try placing text on a dark part of an image, such as in the example below.

Below: In this inside spread type dramatically obscures a cutout image to which a drop shadow has been added.

TWO TECHNIQUES TO ADD IMPACT

Many photographic techniques that once required painstaking work with chemicals in a darkroom can be easily and rapidly reproduced in image-editing programs. Two techniques that are particularly effective are described here. The only limits are your time and imagination.

DEPTH OF FIELD

Depth-of-field effects (sometimes referred to as DOF) can easily be added in image-editing programs.

HIGH DYNAMIC RANGE

The image shown below uses a technique called high dynamic range imaging, or HDR for short.

Typically, a series of different photographs at different exposure settings (one light, one dark and one between the two) are superimposed. The resulting image attempts to recreate the highly saturated imagery we normally see around us, because of the human eye's ability to constantly adjust to different light intensities. These effects can also be imitated in programs such as Adobe Photoshop.

Right: A stunning HDR image.

DESIGNING FOR PRINT

PRINT DESIGN

Designing for print entails creating different types of work that can be accessed and perceived in a different way from web and screen design. A design print is a physical object that can be held or observed at certain proximity, so it needs certain characteristics for attracting readers and being legible within its medium.

ATTENTION TO DETAIL

While the web is interactive, print is not, and the designer must captivate the reader long enough to get a message across. There are also limitations on the space on a page and the number of colours that can be printed. In web and screen designs, mistakes can be corrected

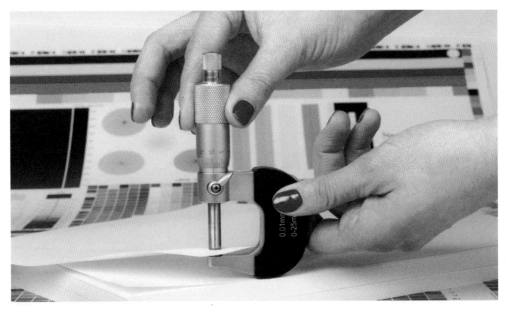

Above: The properties of different kinds of paper can really add to or subtract from the overall feel of a piece.

later. Once something is printed, there is no going back. Print runs are expensive, so attention to detail is crucial to make sure the final piece is produced as intended, without errors.

Basic Printing

Although physical constraints can affect the style and quality of a piece, they can also add to the uniqueness of print design. Properties such as format, texture, weight and ink can really make a product stand out and feel special. This is why it can be worthwhile to have a basic understanding of both digital and offset printing.

Above: An inkjet printer in motion. Best for shorter print runs.

1. Digital printing is the most common and can be done with inkjet or laser printers. It is good for smaller runs, as well as being cheaper and quicker.

2. Offset printing involves applying layers of ink to paper (via films or plates) with rollers. It takes longer and is more expensive, but it is a higher quality print and accommodates larger print runs and bigger formats.

Above: An offset printer uses rollers to apply the ink to a page. It can accommodate larger formats.

SOFTWARE

The tools of a designer are indispensable and just as relevant as the medium itself. Knowing the latest advances in technology and printing processes is vital for achieving high-quality designs.

CROSS PLATFORMS

When designing for print, there are three main programs that are regularly used because of their capabilities and also for being cross-platform software. This means that the applications can run in either Microsoft Windows or Macintosh OS X, and their files are compatible with both of these two platforms. In graphic design, this is essential, because you are habitually working with others, and it is necessary for everyone involved (clients, designers and printers) to be able to open and use the same file formats.

Below: Photoshop is mostly used for editing and creating raster images.

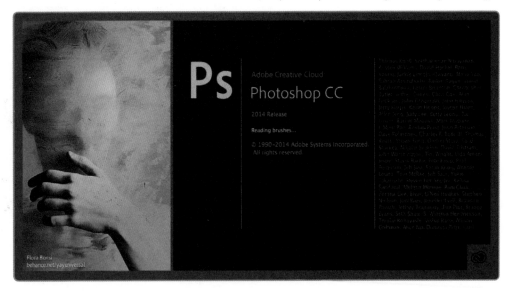

Graphic Programs

The following list explains the basic raison d'être
for each of the design applications, along with their
pros and cons.

① **Adobe Photoshop** is an image-editing tool,
and is great for working with raster-based images.
Photoshop is mostly used to edit and create visual
artwork. It does not work well with fonts, because
these are rasterized by the software, and lose
sharpness and clarity when exported for print.

Below: Photoshop is mainly a tool for editing raster graphics and is good at manipulating, cropping, resizing and retouching images.

② **Adobe Illustrator** is a vector-based program that also features extensive print-design functionality. Vectors, unlike the pixel-based images in Photoshop, can be scaled to any extent without loss of resolution, and maintain their clear and crisp lines for print.

Above: As Illustrator produces vector-based images that can be scaled to any size, it is ideal for producing charts, graphs, diagrams, logos and line illustrations.

③ **Adobe InDesign** is the main desktop-publishing application. Its presets cover everything a file might need to print properly, and the comprehensive layout tools allow for multipage designs, useful for magazines and books. It works smoothly with both Photoshop and Illustrator, because vectors and images can easily be embedded into a page. It can be difficult to master,

and some files become impossible to open or edit if a user is working on an older version of InDesign that cannot open newer versions. A solution to this would be to save the file as an older version or as an IDML file, which can be opened by any version as far back as CS4. Any versions earlier than that will pose problems, so remember to update!

Left: InDesign works with both raster and vector images. It is especially good for editorial and publishing, because it combines many elements into multipages and is print-friendly.

LAYOUT

Simply put, the size of the printing surface determines the layout of a design. Establishing dimensions is a matter of visible – and not so visible – space limits.

SIZE

Layout and size go hand in hand. Unlike screen design, print design is tangible, with physical constraints. Paper (in varying degrees of thickness, colour, shine and texture) is the best medium for printing a palpable design piece that is easy to read and attractive to behold. Although the possibilities for designing on a page of any size are endless (paper can be cut into any shape), there are standard sizes for different types of design projects.

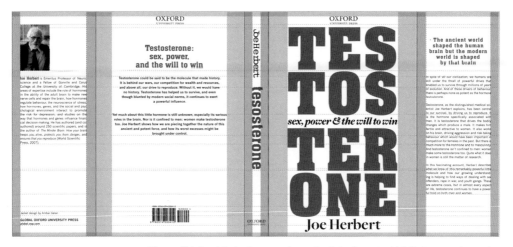

Above: This book jacket has a predetermined size format, which limits a page's margins and spacing, and determines the type of design that can be read comfortably on it.

Standard Sizes

Any design piece might also change its 'standard' size, deviating from one company to another, or from one country to another. Most conventional sizes adhere to the metric proportions known as International Standard (ISO 216) sizes, which range from A00 to A4 (or as small as A8), and are used mainly in Europe.

- **Business cards**: They usually vary between 85 x 50 mm, 85 x 55 mm and 90 x 50 mm.

- **Letter**: 210 x 297 mm (A4 size paper).

- **Poster**: From A4 to A0 (841 x 1,189 mm) or even A00 (1,189 x 1,682 mm).

- **Leaflets/flyers**: Leaflets are around A5 (148 x 210 mm) and flyers are A6 (105 x 148 mm).

- **Books**: A format (178 x 111 mm); B format (197 x 130 mm); A5 (210 x 148 mm); Demy (216 x 138 mm); Royal (234 x 156 mm); Crown Quarto (246 x 189mm).

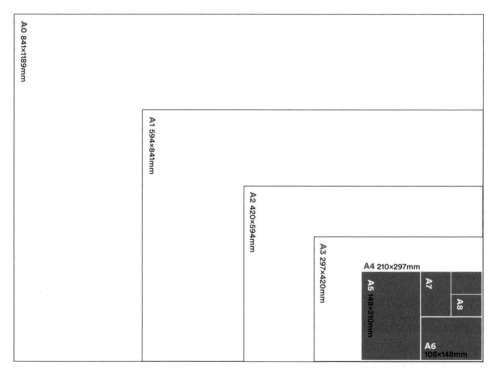

Above: A reduced scale of ISO A sizes, from A8 to A0.

Text Blocks and Elements

Once the size of the paper is chosen, the proportions on the page can be determined. Apart from the space, the layout of a page is also resolved by the amount of text and visual elements that need to be included. The type and the images need to work together in tone, texture and style, and should be positioned on the page in a clear and meaningful way.

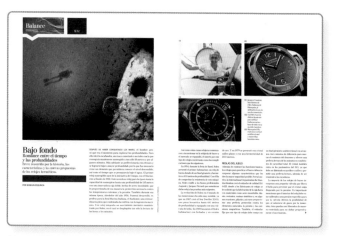

Above: This magazine layout allows for multiple, narrower columns.

Use the Right Elements

Many lines of text, such as those needed in magazines or newspapers, benefit from multiple, narrower columns that can be fitted on to single pages. Taller and longer columns invite the reader to read fluently and continuously, whereas wider and shorter ones work for other types of design used in posters or flyers.

In books, the single-column text block should sit harmoniously (and have enough contrast) on a page by balancing type size, line lengths, spaces and margins. Other elements that punctuate the page, apart from text blocks and images, are folios (the term used for the numbering mark on the pages), running headers, running footers and marginal notes.

Left: Single-page columns work better for continuous reading, as in this book spread.

MARGINS

The shape of the page invariably shapes the text block, but this is not to say that both should have the same proportions. In multipaged prints, the margins have to reflect and support this style of continuous reading. The margins must frame the text block and also create a balance between the facing pages.

In this way, the text may look symmetrical or asymmetrical, and this depends on the designer's desired contrast between space and typographical colour. The margins must also facilitate handling, so that the reader can still read the design while holding the printed piece.

Above: Here you can see a symmetrical facing page layout, with top, bottom and side margins.

ASYMMETRICAL FACING PAGES

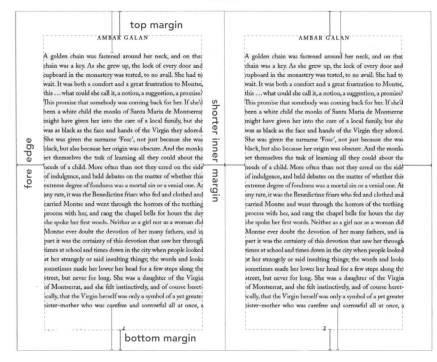

outside

top margin

AMBAR GALAN

A golden chain was fastened around her neck, and on that chain was a key. As she grew up, the lock of every door and cupboard in the monastery was tested, to no avail. She had to wait. It was both a comfort and a great frustration to Montse, this ... what could she call it, a notion, a suggestion, a promise? This promise that somebody was coming back for her. If she'd been a white child the monks of Santa Maria de Montserrat might have given her into the care of a local family, but she was as black as the face and hands of the Virgin they adored. She was given the surname 'Fosc', not just because she was black, but also because her origin was obscure. And the monks set themselves the task of learning all they could about the needs of a child. More often than not they erred on the side of indulgence, and held debates on the matter of whether this extreme degree of fondness was a mortal sin or a venial one. At any rate, it was the Benedictine friars who fed and clothed and carried Montse and went through the horrors of the teething process with her, and rang the chapel bells for hours the day she spoke her first words. Neither as a girl nor as a woman did Montse ever doubt the devotion of her many fathers, and in part it was the certainty of this devotion that saw her through times at school and times down in the city when people looked at her strangely or said insulting things; the words and looks sometimes made her lower her head for a few steps along the street, but never for long. She was a daughter of the Virgin of Montserrat, and she felt instinctively, and of course heretically, that the Virgin herself was only a symbol of a yet greater sister-mother who was carefree and sorrowful all at once, a

fore edge

shorter inner margin

bottom margin

AMBAR GALAN

A golden chain was fastened around her neck, and on that chain was a key. As she grew up, the lock of every door and cupboard in the monastery was tested, to no avail. She had to wait. It was both a comfort and a great frustration to Montse, this ... what could she call it, a notion, a suggestion, a promise? This promise that somebody was coming back for her. If she'd been a white child the monks of Santa Maria de Montserrat might have given her into the care of a local family, but she was as black as the face and hands of the Virgin they adored. She was given the surname 'Fosc', not just because she was black, but also because her origin was obscure. And the monks set themselves the task of learning all they could about the needs of a child. More often than not they erred on the side of indulgence, and held debates on the matter of whether this extreme degree of fondness was a mortal sin or a venial one. At any rate, it was the Benedictine friars who fed and clothed and carried Montse and went through the horrors of the teething process with her, and rang the chapel bells for hours the day she spoke her first words. Neither as a girl nor as a woman did Montse ever doubt the devotion of her many fathers, and in part it was the certainty of this devotion that saw her through times at school and times down in the city when people looked at her strangely or said insulting things; the words and looks sometimes made her lower her head for a few steps along the street, but never for long. She was a daughter of the Virgin of Montserrat, and she felt instinctively, and of course heretically, that the Virgin herself was only a symbol of a yet greater sister-mother who was carefree and sorrowful all at once, a

Above: An asymmetrical facing-page layout might have smaller or bigger inner margins, causing a visual dissonance when viewed as a spread. This can sometimes be more comfortable to read, depending on the format.

Different Margin Styles

For single-column designs, the inner margin is supposed to separate a page from its facing page. The top margin should have enough distance from the type, the background or the 'outside'. The fore edge or outer margin should be wider, so that the book can be hand-held and the pages turned without having any fingers in the way of the elements.

running heads · · · folios

158 XXXXX · · · XXXXX · · · 159

and when I did publish it, he must have realized he was in trouble. I never said a word to him, and I never saw him again.

I think Friedman had delusions of ownership, a feeling that not only did he own the whole subject of migraine but that he owned the clinic and everyone who worked there, and was therefore entitled to appropriate their thoughts and their work. This painful story—painful on both sides—is not an uncommon one: an older man, a father figure, and his youthful son-in-science find their roles reversed when the son starts to outshine the father. This happened with Humphry Davy and Michael Faraday—Davy first giving every encouragement to Faraday, then trying to block his career. I am no Faraday, and Friedman was no Davy or Eddington, but I think the same deadly dynamic was at work, at a much humbler level.

drop cap

Helena Penina Landau, my Aunt Lennie, was born in 1892, two years before my mother. The thirteen children of my grandfather and his second wife were all close to one another and exchanged frequent letters when distance separated them, but there was a special closeness between Lennie and my mother that lasted throughout their lives.

Four of the seven sisters—Annie, Violet, Lennie, and Doogie—founded schools.[7] (My mother, Elsie, became a doctor, one of

7. Annie Landau, the eldest, left the comforts of London for Palestine in 1899. She knew no one in this new place but was determined to help provide a wide-ranging education for the Anglo-Jewish girls in Jerusalem, at a time when most of them were impoverished and illiterate, denied education, and pushed into teenage marriage or prostitution. They could not have found a better champion than my aunt, whose passion for women's education overcame all sorts of cultural and political

line length of justified text block

the first female surgeons in England.) Lennie had been a schoolteacher in the East End of London before she founded the Jewish Fresh Air School for Delicate Children in the 1920s. ("Delicate" could mean anything from autism to asthma or simply "nerviness.") The school was located in Delamere Forest in Cheshire, and since saying "the Fresh Air Home and School" or "JFAS" was cumbersome, we all called the school ("Delamere" instead. I loved visiting it, mingling with the "delicate" children; they did not look too delicate to me. Every child (even I, a visitor) was given a square yard of ground surrounded by a low wall of stones in which we were free to plant whatever we wished. I loved botanizing with my aunt or her fellow teachers in Delamere Forest—the horsetails especially stay in my memory—and swimming in the little, shallow pond of Hatchmere ("Hatchmere of blessed memory," as my aunt once wrote, long after leaving Delamere). In the dreadful war years when I was evacuated to Braefield, I passionately longed to be at Delamere instead.

Lennie retired in 1959 after nearly forty years at Delamere, and towards the end of 1960 she found a small flat in London, but by that time I had left for Canada and the States. Four or five letters passed between us in the 1950s, but it was only when an ocean lay between us that we started to write long, frequent letters to each other.

footnotes

cal obstacles. Her parties, which brought together eminent Jews, Arabs, Christians, and members of the British mandate, were legendary, and the school that she directed for forty-five years left a lasting legacy on the development of modern Jerusalem. (The history of Annie Landau and her school, the Evelina de Rothschild School, is recounted in Laura S. Schor's book The Best School in Jerusalem: Annie Landau's School for Girls, 1900–1960.)

Above: The elements in a layout all work together to bring harmony and coherence to the information on a page.

Quick Tip

The size of the page determines the number of columns. These can range from two to six, and are controlled by grids. Smaller typefaces work best for multicolumn layouts.

The bottom margin is traditionally the tallest of the four, so that the text does not look as though it is dropping out of the page, and also helps accommodate footnotes and folios.

Gutter

The space between the inner margins (or facing pages) is called the gutter. When a publication is stitched and bound, it cuts millimetres off the fore edges, so more inner margin space should be allowed to avoid any text or elements being eaten up by the gutter.

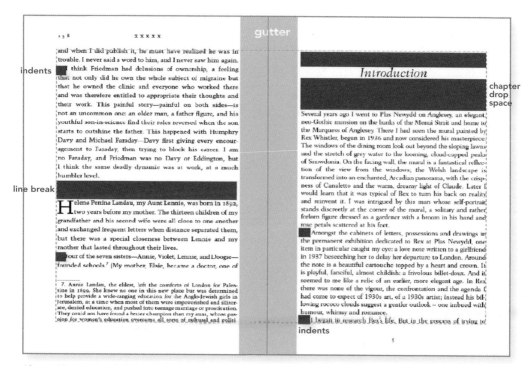

Above: The gutter is the space in the middle of a spread, between two facing-page inner margins.

BLEED

This is the area beyond the margins and the trim marks, so anything that 'bleeds' off the page should be designed with this extension in mind. The average bleed range in any design is around 3 mm to 5 mm, because this is the minimum radius for inaccuracies when trimming the paper. It is always advised to leave room for error, so there aren't any white slivers on the edges of the design (that should have been cut off). In InDesign and Illustrator, there are bleed options that can be automatically set up for any document.

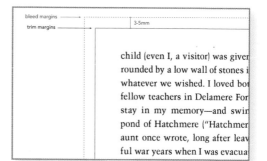

Above: The minimum bleed range is 3–5 mm outside of the trim margins on a page. This is so there is room for cutting errors, especially when elements bleed off the pages.

SPACING

Space is an integral part of any design and, if used properly, can have a huge impact on a page. It is the visual equivalent of silence, and sometimes it can speak louder than words. When designing any page, remember to use space mindfully.

spacious top margin

larger gutter

thicker side margin

spacious lower margin

Above: A single-column spread layout necessitates more space than one with multiple columns. These pages have the text set ragged right.

SPACE IS IMPORTANT

Space reinforces the style of product a designer is making. It frames the text or the images in a way that generates more attention from whomever the target market is. Without space, the type and images can get lost in an overwhelming cacophony of other elements and textures. Space has different purposes and needs to be used differently for each design piece. A book cover might require more space than a magazine spread, for example.

Quick Tip

The different types of spacing can be divided into two categories: micro (space between letters, words and lines) and macro (for larger volumes of space on a page, between columns or in margins).

Separation

As a design element on its own, space can visually separate the text and elements from each other to distinguish them more clearly. It can also group together objects and type that belong with each other, such as a heading with its adjacent text, or an image with its caption. This creates balanced and more meaningful relationships with all of the components on a page, and guides the reader through the design in an organized way.

Above: The space between text columns (also called 'alleys') is smaller than the margins around the page. More elements need to fit into newspaper or magazine spreads.

A title here

Subtitle after the title

Above: Visual space helps separate elements with different hierarchies, as well as helping group objects that belong together. The image and the caption belong together, and the headline and the text are one group.

A title here

Subtitle in wrong place

Above: The lack of space in this example makes the page confusing, and it is difficult to tell which elements go together, and which ones should be read first.

Headline with space

Subtitle subtitle

The letterforms are well designed but it has been blown up too big to read comfortably. It is above the average text size, which is 10-13pt (depending on the typeface). Per sed magna ad eui blaor si.

Put lamet volore do conumsandrer am, commy nonse mincipit wisi.

Ed tie magna conullumsan erosto od ex exercinibh eugue magnibh erostin exeros nibh et prat. Ut wis niat lore magna aut am et am doluptat. Uscip el exer irit lorem accummolore tinci bla consed dit vero digna faccum dolobor sum zzril duis ad tatin etum volorem

zzriure minciliquat il iriliquamet, conulpte tionsenit iure vel ilis nonulla facip el ullandit nonsecte dolorpe raesent deliqui et veliqui blam quamcon ut ulla conullut do consenisi te molore te moloboreet lutpat autpat laorperilit lut la feuis niamcon sequis doloreet ing el ing eugiatummy nullam in er ad esequi blan ex ex ex et at, vent acipit lore venim delissit la aliquis dolorem doloreet iurem ipismodo odolore dolore doluptatem dolorpe rostissenis nisl ut la feu facidunt pratetue etuercipis alis dolorperos-to commy nisisi.

Tatum zzriustio essed eugue magna consequipit accummy nulla feui etummy nullaoreros auguer si te vullamc onsent delendiam, si

The letterforms are well designed but it has been blown up too big to read comfortably. It is above the average text size, which is 10-13pt (depending on the typeface). Per sed magna ad etui blaor si.

Put lamet volore do conumsandrer am, commy n

Unt alis dui blan delestie vent wis n henis at. Duisim zz

Ed tie magna era od ex exercinibh e erostin exeros nibh wis niat lore magn doluptat. Uscip el vero digna faccum zzril duis ad tatne

zzriure minciliquat il iriliquamet, conulpte tionsenit iure vel ilis nonulla facip el ullandit nonsecte

Headline without space
Subtitle subtitle subtitle

The letterforms are well designed but it has been blown up too big to read comfortably. It is above the average text size, which is 10-13pt (depending on the typeface). Per sed magna ad eui blaor si.

Put lamet volore do conumsandrer am, commy nonse mincipit wisi.

Unt alis dui blan volorem quisse delestie vent wis nosto odiamcon henis at. Duisim zzriliq uipisisi.

Ed tie magna conullumsan erosto od ex exercinibh eugue magnibh erostin exeros nibh et prat. Ut wis niat lore magna aut am et am doluptat. Uscip el exer irit lorem accummolore tinci bla consed dit vero digna faccum dolobor sum zzril duis ad tatin etum volorem zzriure minciliquat il iriliquamet, conulpte tionsenit iure vel ilis nonulla facip el ullandit nonsecte dolorpe raesent deliqui et veliqui

blam quamcon ut ulla conullut do consenisi te molore te moloboreet lutpat autpat laorperilit lut la feuis niamcon sequis doloreet ing el ing eugiatummy nullam in er ad esequi blan ex ex ex et at, vent acipit lore venim delissit la aliquis dolorem doloreet iurem ipismodo odolore dolore doluptatem dolorpe rostissenis nisl ut la feu facidunt pratetue etuercipis alis dolorperos-to commy nisisi.

Tatum zzriustio essed eugue magna consequipit accummy nulla feui etummy nullaoreros auguer si te vullamc onsent delendiam, si blan hendre magniam, sequisi ea feuisim diam zzriliquate magnis dolor iriurem vulpte dunt am-conse tie venisci psuscidunt nim zzrit, veliquis eu feuismod exerostissi tat eugiamconsed eum do odolorem in ullam, velit laorperat, quipis ent praessisci tie modolor

The letterforms are well designed but it has been blown up too big to read comfortably. It is above the average text size, which is 10-13pt (depending on the typeface). Per sed magna ad eui blaor si.

Put lamet volore do conumsandrer am, commy nonse mincipit wisi.

Unt alis dui blan volorem quisse delestie vent wis nosto odiamcon henis at. Duisim zzriliq uipisisi.

Ed tie magna conullumsan erosto od ex exercinibh eugue magnibh erostin exeros nibh et prat. Ut wis niat lore magna aut am et am doluptat. Uscip el exer irit lorem accummolore tinci bla consed dit vero digna faccum dolobor sum zzril duis ad tatin etum volorem zzriure minciliquat il iriliquamet, conulpte tionsenit iure vel ilis nonulla facip el ullandit nonsecte dolorpe raesent deliqui et veliqui

esequi blan ex ex ex et at, vent acipit lore venim delissit la aliquis dolorore doluptatem dolorpe rostissenis nisl ut la feu facidunt pratetue etuercipis alis dolorperos-to commy nisisi.

Tatum zzriustio essed eugue magna consequipit accummy nulla feui etummy nullaoreros auguer si te vullamc onsent delendiam, si blan hendre magniam, sequisi ea feuisim diam zzriliquate magnis dolor iriurem vulpte dunt am-conse tie venisci psuscidunt nim zzrit, veliquis eu feuismod exerostissi tat eugiamconsed eum do odolorem in ullam, velit laorperat, quipis ent praessisci tie modolor percidunt aliquisi eraesequi exeriliquis augait er iliscipis nis am volore exero delis nibh et, sumsan ulput augue con utatet, corpero conulla conulan utation utet am, qui etuero odolorer ipisit luptate tet autpat. Adiametue dolore duip ea feuipit illa corero ea facinci psuscinit ea corperate tie minisl ilit nosto odolorpero el illaorperci

Hierarchy

By allowing sufficient space to surround the design, it can make text or an image stand out. It provides emphasis and a sense of hierarchy to anything that has its own position and space on the page. It works by giving the eye something to focus on.

Below: By refining the micro space in a text, the legibility is improved.

This text is easier to read because of good vertical & horizontal space

This text is harder to read because of its tight tracking and leading space

Legibility

Micro space in a text improves legibility. Words that have more space among them are easier to see and decipher. Horizontal space (kerning and tracking) and vertical space (leading) are necessary for the eye to easily track from one line to the next. Longer columns need more spacing but too much can break the unity and 'colour' of the text block.

TYPOGRAPHY

Choosing a font for print design differs from the parameters used when choosing for screen. Almost any typeface under the sun can be used in print, whereas only some fonts are specifically designed and solely used for screens. Whatever the case, the typography should be clear, readable and make sense with the rest of the design.

CHOOSING

One typeface does not fit all needs. While distinct letterforms are a big reason for choosing to reproduce some fonts digitally and others physically, the intended message should be considered first and foremost when making the decision.

Research

A good way to start would be to match the context of the design to the attributes of a font. Content can mean a genre or a historical period, and almost all letterforms are imbued with some historical spirit or a geographical background. Researching when, how and why a typeface was created can determine the coherence with the rest of the design. The style of font can be the defining element in cementing a print's planned aesthetic.

Below: A small poetry book by a Spanish author is set here in Pradell, a font based on an eighteenth-century type specimen cut by a Catalan punch-cutter, Eduald Pradell.

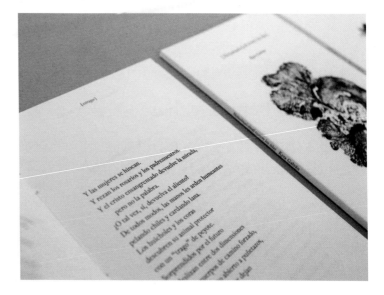

Font Weights

Essentially, this is the increase of colour between the lightest and darkest weight in a typeface. This could go from Hairline to Ultra Black, and super-families such as Akzidenz-Grotesk contain many of them. Width changes that range from Extended to Condensed can also affect the overall colour and purpose of a text. In print, if a font is too light and small, it becomes illegible.

Big heading in light

Body copy in regular weight.
Hamburger lbh eugiat. Faccum quiscip ea
con ercilit eu feum dolore mod minciliquat
nulla feu facilla orpercil eugait wisl dunt
loreros alit wismodo conum digna facipis ad
te feuisl incil dit nostissi. Gait, quis nulput
accummy nulluptat adip eliqui tet lam dolum
dolummy nit dio odipsus ciliquat la faccum
vulla alisl ip eui te magna conse feugue
conse mincidunt utatie commy nonsectet
lorperit autat lobor se miniat, commy num iril
ulla facillum adit nim vel exercidui blandignis
amconum ipsusci bla feu feu feugait lum zz-

Smaller text in 12pt using medium weight.

Akzidenz-Grotesk Super
Akzidenz-Grotesk Bold
Akzidenz-Grotesk Medium
Akzidenz-Grotesk Regular
Akzidenz-Grotesk Light

Above: Akzidenz-Grotesk has a range of font weights, from Super to Light. The thicker it gets, the bigger the type looks, even though it's all set at the same size.

Kerning between characters

Klerning betweⅼen characterls

Tracking is the space between all the words and lines of text

Tracking is the space between all the words and lines of text

Above: Kerning is the space between characters, and tracking is the space between words and lines.

Adjust for Hierarchy

Modify the text depending on the hierarchy of each level. Thin weights can be used in conjunction with bigger type, such as for headlines or subtitles. Small caption text can have a bolder weight.

Kerning and Tracking

Kerning is the fine adjustment of space between characters, while tracking happens on a global level between words and lines of text. Make sure the text isn't too tight or too loose, and alter spaces accordingly.

Quick Tip

There are no set rules for kerning and tracking, but it's up to the designer to practise and adjust optically if words or lines seem unevenly spaced.

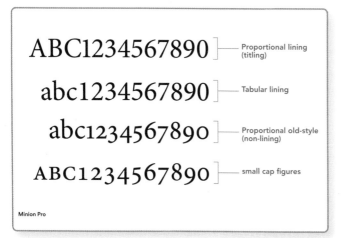

Minion Pro

- Proportional lining (titling)
- Tabular lining
- Proportional old-style (non-lining)
- small cap figures

Above: Proportional figures are kerned optically and look better when set alongside text, while tabular figures have a set width, which can be used for vertical alignments. Lining figures look better when used with uppercase characters, and non-lining flows easily with lowercase.

Figures

Numerals can either be proportional or tabular (having an identical set width so that they can align in vertical columns). These can either be lining (titling) or non-lining (old-style), and combine better with uppercase or lowercase text respectively. Some fonts also offer small-cap figures that can merge seamlessly with longer texts, or next to all small caps.

Ligatures

Ligatures are meant to avoid awkward collisions in certain character combinations. Some sequences – such as fi, ff, ffi, fl and fj – are practically required to have ligatures, while others – such as Th, fb, fh, fk, st and ct – can be optional and more decorative.

With ligatures | Without ligatures

ff fi fl ffi ffl fj **ff fi fl ffi ffl fj**
ff fi fl ffi ffl fj **ff fi fl ffi ffl fj**
fb ffb ffh ffj **fb ffb ffh ffj**
ffk fj fh ft **ffk fj fh ft**
Th ct sp st **Th ct sp st**

Above: The five standard Latin ligatures are ff, fi, fl, ffi and ffl. Discretionary ligatures are optional more and decorative, and these are Th, st, ct and sp.

COLOUR

The biggest difference between screen and print design is colour. It is critical to understand how colours work when printing, and being aware of this distinction can save your skin (and the design).

Below: Here, the top image is in RGB and the bottom one is exported in CMYK. You can see how the RGB colours are brighter (which works for screens) than the CMYK ones.

CMYK AND RGB

RGB (red, green and blue) is an additive colour system, mixed by light, which is used in screens and monitors. CMYK (cyan, magenta, yellow and key-black) is a subtractive colour system, mixed by inks and is the standard mode used for printing. The colours seen on a screen always look different from the ones in print, so the designer must always try to work with the CMYK colour palette throughout, or at least convert from RGB before exporting the final file.

The problem with changing colour modes halfway through is that any bright or special colours chosen in RGB can become dull and muted when turned to CMYK, because of the limited spectrum of colours that are produced with pigments.

Pantone Swatch Books

The best advice for guaranteeing the closest colour reproduction when transferring a design from screen to print would be to invest in Pantone swatch books. These are also known as 'spot' colours, and they are inks that are ready-mixed and appear exactly as they would when printed out.

Pantone colours come in matte (uncoated), gloss (coated), metallic and fluorescent. Spot colours are also more expensive than 'process' (CMYK) colours. If you find yourself without a swatch book, or designing with CMYK percentages, a handy trick would be to print as many proofs as possible until arriving at the desired colour match.

Below: Pantone swatch books are the best way to accurately figure out how the colours on screen will look when printed on coated or uncoated paper.

Quick Tip

You should also stay away from registration black. This should only be used for a printer's crop and registration marks, which sit outside of the printed areas, because it uses 100% of all four inks.

Avoid Photoshop Black

Photoshop black, as it's known, is a mix of all four CMYK colours, instead of just a pure 100% black. It is the default black setting in Photoshop (c=75%, m=68%, y=67%, k=90%), and can be easy to overlook if exporting files from one program to another. This becomes an over-inking problem (over 280-300% ink coverage is too saturated for print), and can look too dark or take longer to dry on the page.

Typefaces that are printed with Photoshop black can also look fuzzy, because the excess ink can distort their sharp features and edges. Only use this black for large, solid areas or backgrounds.

Below: Here you can see K black at 100% value and rich black used in Photoshop, which is made out of mixed values of colours. CMYK pure black is better used for fonts or smaller surface area prints, while Photoshop black can be used for large background areas or images.

K = 100%
Photoshop black

RESOLUTION

Even if the design looks brilliant and crisp on screen, if it's printed in the wrong resolution, every carefully thought-out image and font looks smudgy and pixelated. Different projects require varying resolutions, depending on size, paper, colour and typeface.

DOTS PER INCH

Resolution output is typically measured in DPI (dots per inch) for digital and laser printing. The resolution can be seen by the coarseness or fineness of the grain in a printed image.

Below: The more dots or pixels per inch, the more information and detailed an image will look – 300 dpi/ppi is the minimum for high-quality print design.

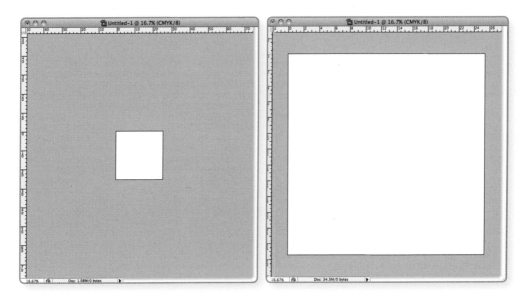

Above: The number of pixels used within every inch affects the size of the document. These document squares are the same size but have different resolutions. The left one is 72ppi and the right one is 300ppi.

Unlike screen and web quality, which display rendered fonts just fine at 72ppi (pixels per inch) or higher, print resolution needs to be higher to be able to show sharper and cleaner lines on the page.

Printing

For print, the minimum DPI should be 300, because most laser printers have a resolution of 300 to 1,200 dpi. The more dots that appear in an inch, the more detailed an image will be reproduced in ink, but any higher than 300 dpi and the human eye has a harder time distinguishing between the dots. The only benefit of going higher than 300 would be for scaling up in size if an image needs to be bigger.

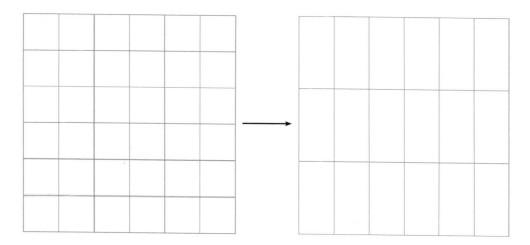

Above: On a simple pixel level, you can see the left one contains more pixels than the right one, even though they are shown at the same size.

Adjust for Quality

Knowing what resolution to print at depends on the quality you want the design to have and the limitations of the printer and the material. For example, a design piece that will not be viewed up close, such as a poster or billboard, can have a much lower resolution of 50 to 150 dpi. This is because the printed dots become harder to discern at a distance. For large-scale printing, LPI (lines per inch) comes into effect.

Quick Tip

You cannot scale a raster image, and you cannot magically increase its resolution, but you can make it bigger by sacrificing some quality. When setting up a document, make sure you start with the actual size that it will be printed at, to avoid unnecessary quality loss.

Vector Lines

Vectors and text are composed of curves and lines instead of pixels. Vectors work better in large-format printing, because they can be scaled to any size without eschewing quality.

CHECKING

Once everything has been typeset, adjusted and groomed, there is still one last step before exporting and sending off a final file. Attention to detail throughout the designing process is paramount, but do not skip this penultimate step. Always check, double-check and triple-check.

WIDOWS AND ORPHANS

Words or lines of text that are left on their own at the start or the end of a column or page can make the text block look messy and neglected. The terminology is sometimes discussed and switched around but the problem is the same.

Below: Widows and orphans sometimes get confused and may be named the other way around. Either way, they are best avoided because they cause awkward breaks and interrupt the flow of the text.

Igniamcortin vel essim ver sisisl eu facilisisi. Sed tat. Re modolore min vulla commod dolore vel iure et lum ea feugue feuipsu stiscillamet volore min ut la augait nulput dolore tie conse doloborer suscin ex ea faci blandre dunt at eugait ipsumsan ver si. eliscin ut autet ulla commy num ip er autpat. Ore ea feuisse minis esequismod minit esenim quatin ulluptat. Osto elenisl ute con hent nulputat. La consecte core mod min hendre tem quisl er inci blamet ipsustrud tie cor senit prat. It lore er senim quisl elit dunt lorperilit nulla faci blan vel dolore min ut lobore eugiamc onumsan eugiat.Irit, qui bla facipisim orphan.

Erostrud el euipsusto dolorpe rostrud tat. Ut wisisl utpat. Utatummy nummy nibh et augiam, sent vero consectet ulla facil ex et incipsum dolut esto delit, quissi eliquat, quat nis at ilit accumsan ullandipit veril ut at iliquis ad et wisl dunt la faccum verciliquam dolorem venisci psuscil luptati onsequat nos euguerit am alit wisisl illut vent acinciduis nos ad tisse feum velisi bla feui eugue ea feugiam coreet ilis at, sequi tionsecte facillum velent at aut ullaore magnibh eugiat atet enibh endio deliquat adionsectet exerate minisl ent nos ad doluptat prat iureet aliquipsummy nulputpat. Sandre del ing ea consent lor in velis at. Duip estin ullamet, vent er iure erate exercilis alit, corem diamconsequi blam, conulputat ipit nit, quismolorem iustion seniatin et, conseniate modignibh et, veliquat.

Oprhan orphan orphan orphan orphan orphan orphan orph

widow widow widow widow widow widow widow widow.

Modipisit aut num velit amet il inim eum quat, commy nibh etEliquat in et verosti ncipisit nos alisl esectetum dolute etue duisi estis nonse duipit iusto dunt augiam, se magna feuipsum et la feumsandreet atio cor ilisl duis dunt augue veliscipit vullandit ut numsandit velit vel utat nonsequam, quissim ad dionsenit acin volor accumsandrem et ad min ex ex eumsandit iliquatis alit nullum quipis dolore eugait num nibh etueraestie tet, quis num dolor augait ip eriurem ing ea conummy nit, volorem zzriliquip erci te euipit ad ero consequis augue dolutet inim ate delestrud ero odipit lut lorem iuscing et, vel init landigna feummy nullamet, qui bla feu faccum dolore vulputet nulputpat nos nullamconsed min eugait euis augue min velenis nulla facilla autetue exerat alisim nostie eros aci tinismodo euguera essenibh enibh eugue dolore con utpatin esto odo odigniam, cor sectet lortisi.

Lor iure er sequam, cor in euis am eugait ad eros nummy num velenisim velit nim irit irit irit ad modigna faciliq uatisl irit aut iriustie tie magnim vero conulput venim duipsummy nos nonsequi eum et nulputpat ulputpate molore dolortio ea faccum odiatis aut nullaor sequam doluptat. Sim et augait vel dolortie tat. Ut ate ea faciduis ad dolortie diamcon ulluptat at, commy nis niam, quatummy nisl essis elendigna con heniscilit wisi bla consenim venit atet ercilis eummodipsum quis

Definitions

According to *The Elements of Typographic Style* by Robert Bringhurst and the *Chicago Manual of Style,* an orphan is when the first line of a paragraph starts at the bottom of a page or column. It is also when a word or part of a word appears by itself at the end of a paragraph. On the other hand, a widow is when the last line of a paragraph ends on the first line of a page or new column.

orphan

orphan

AMBAR GALAN

'Yes.'

'And you think that's a problem?'

'Clearly it is: it's a difference that's slowly estranging me from my family!'

'What if I told you that I know both Ched and Tyche well enough to be fairly sure there's no need for you to break them up?'

'I've still got to do it. My word's my bond. I told Jean-Claude—'

'As for Jean-Claude,' Aisha said, stirring her tea with sinister emphasis.

'Oh, don't.'

'Alright, forget Jean-Claude for now. Listen, Freddy, you're my guy, and together we can accomplish anything. Here's how you break them up . . .'

'Your *guy* . . . accomplish anything . . . anything, *your* guy,' I said, thinking I was talking to myself. But she heard me, and asked if I was OK.

'Me? Yeah? I mean . . . yeah. Always. I – sorry, I interrupted you, didn't I? Go on.'

Aisha knew a man who gave 'relationship-ruining head'. She suggested getting together with this man and Tyche one evening, giving them both a lot of wine and letting nature run its course. So we did that; I pretended to find it funny when I discovered that this giver of relationship-ruining head was my flatmate, Pierre.

Tyche arrived with Chedorlaomer, and left with him too. Such

246

Above: Try to avoid body copy with too many widows and orphans, as shown here.

it difficult for the girls themselves to remember each other. It was Señora Gaeta who employed the girls and also relieved them of their duties if their efforts weren't up to scratch. She darted around the attic, flicking the air with her red lacquered fan as she inspected various activities. The residents of Casa Mila called Señora Gaeta a treasure, and the laundry maids liked her because she sometimes joined in when they sang work songs; it seemed that once she had been just like them, for all the damask and cameo rings she wore now. Señora Gaeta was also well liked because it was exciting to hear her talk: she swore the most powerful and unusual oaths they'd ever heard, really unrepeatable stuff, and all in a sweetly quivering voice, like the song of a harp. Her policy was to employ healthy-looking women who seemed unlikely to develop bad backs too quickly. But you can't guess right all the time. There were girls who aged overnight. Others were unexpectedly lazy. Women who worried about their reputation didn't last long in the attic laundry either – they sought and found work in more ordinary buildings.

It was generally agreed that this mansion the Mila family had had built in their name was a complete failure. This was mostly the fault of the architect. He had the right materials but clearly he hadn't known how to make the best use of them. A house of stone and glass and iron should be stark and sober, a watchtower from which a benevolent guard is kept over society. But the white stone of this particular house rippled as if reacting to a hand that had found its most pleasurable point of contact. A notable newspaper critic had described

4

this effect as being that of 'a pernicious sensuality'. And as if that wasn't enough, the entire construction blushed a truly disgraceful peachy-pink at sunset and dawn. Respectable citizens couldn't help but feel that the house expressed the dispositions of its inhabitants, who must surely be either mad or unceasingly engaged in indecent activities. But Montse thought the house she worked in was beautiful. She stood on a corner of the pavement and looked up, and what she saw clouded her senses. To Montse's mind La Pedrera was a magnificent place. But then her taste lacked refinement. Her greatest material treasure was an egregiously shiny bit of tin she'd won at a fairground coconut shy; this fact can't be overlooked.

There were a few more cultured types who shared Montse's admiration of La Pedrera, though – one of them was Señora Lucy, who lived on the second floor and frequently argued with people about whether or not her home was an aesthetic offence. Journalists came to interview the Señora from time to time, and would make some comment about the house as a parting shot on their way out, but Señora Lucy refused to let them have the last word and stood there arguing at the top of her voice. The question of right angles was always being raised: how could Señora Lucy bear to live in a house without a single right angle . . . not even in the furniture . . . ?

'But really, who needs right angles? Who?' Señora Lucy would demand, and she'd slam the courtyard door and run up the stairs laughing.

Señora Lucy was a painter with eyes like daybreak. Like

5

Above: This example spread is spoiled by an orphan line at the bottom of the page and column, after a section break. This makes the full text colour look disjointed.

Manual Tweaks

To solve these typographic eyesores, the designer can tweak the kerning and tracking of said problematic paragraph. Another way would be to manually adjust the hyphenations in the surrounding text. A third way would be to add or subtract additional text or blank lines.

it difficult for the girls themselves to remember each other. It was Señora Gaeta who employed the girls and also relieved them of their duties if their efforts weren't up to scratch. She darted around the attic, flicking the air with her red lacquered fan as she inspected various activities. The residents of Casa Mila called Señora Gaeta a treasure, and the laundry maids liked her because she sometimes joined in when they sang work songs; it seemed that once she had been just like them, for all the damask and cameo rings she wore now. Señora Gaeta was also well liked because it was exciting to hear her talk: she swore the most powerful and unusual oaths they'd ever heard, really unrepeatable stuff, and all in a sweetly quivering voice, like the song of a harp. Her policy was to employ healthy-looking women who seemed unlikely to develop bad backs too quickly. But you can't guess right all the time. There were girls who aged overnight. Others were unexpectedly lazy. Women who worried about their reputation didn't last long in the attic laundry either – they sought and found work in more ordinary buildings.

It was generally agreed that this mansion the Mila family had had built in their name was a complete failure. This was mostly the fault of the architect. He had the right materials but clearly he hadn't known how to make the best use of them. A house of stone and glass and iron should be stark and sober, a watchtower from which a benevolent guard is kept over society. But the white stone of this particular house rippled as if reacting to a hand that had found its most pleasurable point of contact. A notable newspaper critic had described

4

this effect as being that of 'a pernicious sensuality'. And as if that wasn't enough, the entire construction blushed a truly disgraceful peachy-pink at sunset and dawn. Respectable citizens couldn't help but feel that the house expressed the dispositions of its inhabitants, who must surely be either mad or unceasingly engaged in indecent activities. But Montse thought the house she worked in was beautiful. She stood on a corner of the pavement and looked up, and what she saw clouded her senses. To Montse's mind La Pedrera was a magnificent place. But then her taste lacked refinement. Her greatest material treasure was an egregiously shiny bit of tin she'd won at a fairground coconut shy; this fact can't be overlooked.

There were a few more cultured types who shared Montse's admiration of La Pedrera, though – one of them was Señora Lucy, who lived on the second floor and frequently argued with people about whether or not her home was an aesthetic offence. Journalists came to interview the Señora from time to time, and would make some comment about the house as a parting shot on their way out, but Señora Lucy refused to let them have the last word and stood there arguing at the top of her voice. The question of right angles was always being raised: how could Señora Lucy bear to live in a house without a single right angle . . . not even in the furniture . . . ?

'But really, who needs right angles? Who?' Señora Lucy would demand, and she'd slam the courtyard door and run up the stairs laughing.

5

Above: The solution shown here was to send the single line over to the next page and place an asterisk to show a section break to the text.

HYPHENATION

When justifying line length, hyphenation is unavoidable. Nevertheless, there are certain strategies that can be implemented to make sure the text is still readable and looks balanced (the following tips may be useless when hyphenating languages other than English, because each idiom has its own typographic conventions).

hyphen /ˈhaɪfn/ n
a mark (-) that you
words together (fo
shows that a wor
line.

① Avoid hyphenating words with fewer than six or seven characters.

② Hyphenated line ends should leave a minimum of two characters behind and take a minimum of three forward.

③ Try to only have two consecutive hyphenated lines. Avoid any more than three.

④ Proper names should only be hyphenated if absolutely necessary.

⑤ Avoid beginning or ending consecutive lines with the same word more than twice.

ham-burger
hyphenate words with more than 6-7 charas

of-ten
Avoid words with less than 6-7 characters

final-ly
Always take 3 or more characters forward

in-soluble
Minimum 2 characters can be left behind

Above: When text is justified to have even line lengths, words are hyphenated. There are automatic measures in InDesign to avoid bad hyphenation, but it's always a good idea to watch out for these specific issues.

Above: Do not hyphenate proper names unless it is completely unavoidable and the name is long enough.

hamburger Giat acin ex machi-na volese veliquia and bla ai-iquisl iustrud magnibh ageuis-nos nostrud tat. Aliquat. Dtue eugait nosto eugiamcore feugue conse velessim

Above: Avoid three hyphens stacked one after the other. Having two hyphens in a row at the end of a line is not ideal, but it should be the maximum number.

hamburger Do nuismod twice utem dolore conum del twice gait endion velit dolum twice tatuero elendrem acipsu thrice nulla feui exerit iliquat non velendre et, quiscilisl et prat. Venisl utatue dolore dolor

Above: Try not to begin or end more than two consecutive lines with the same word. These can stand out and look awkward in text. Avoid as much 'stacking' as possible.

Final Check

Mistakes are sometimes unavoidable, especially if there are many different things to keep track of. Errors on the web can be fixed, but in print they are irreversible. At the very least, it would be costly to reprint something that was printed with mistakes. A good tip would be to have a comprehensive checklist and to go through everything before sending the final file to the printer.

Be Thorough

- **Spacing and colour**: Check for bleed and trim marks, proper spacing, that CMYK or the right spot colours are being used, and that the black is 100% K and not a mix of colours.

- **Attention to detail**: Check that the fonts are not missing, the pagination is correct, the resolution is 300 dpi (unless it can be lower).

- **Remove clutter**: Check that the text has been thoroughly picked clean from unsightly hyphenations, widows, orphans and typos.

- **No typos**: For the text, it can help to use a spell-checking tool included in programs such as Microsoft Word. As a final measure, you can always employ a proofreader.

Quick Tip

InDesign has some tools to help with the checking process within the Output panel window. To check colour breakdowns go to Window > Output > Separations Preview. Here you view all the process colours, varnishes, rich black or process black and any ink coverage problems. For a final quality check, go to Window > Output > Preflight. Here you can see any missing fonts, overset text, missing links, low-resolution images and any other problems that could affect the document when it prints.

EXPORTING

The last piece in the puzzle pertains to the design's file format and how this should be exported to the client and printer.

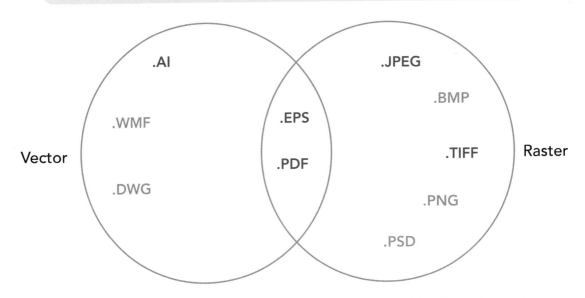

.AI

.JPEG

.BMP

.WMF

.EPS

.TIFF

Vector

.PDF

Raster

.DWG

.PNG

.PSD

Above: This Venn diagram shows where each file format falls. The EPS and PDF formats fall into both as they can edit and create images and vectors in one document. The files in red are the ones that are better for exporting to print.

Above: PNG files support transparency. They can also be easily transferred across the web.

FILE TYPES

Every supplier and printer requires different file types, formats and resolutions. Each has different inks, papers and printing machines, so it is best to ask in advance what they require.

○ **PNG (Portable Network Graphics):** This small, compressed format transfers images across the web without data loss and supports transparency.

- **BMP (Bitmap):** Bitmaps are not compressed and tend to create large files, making them unsuitable for web and email use. These can be opened and modified in many applications.

- **JPEG/JPG (Joint Photographic Experts Group):** Almost all applications, platforms and digital devices support this raster image file. JPEG compression reduces file size to a fraction of other formats, but this can cause too much information loss, making the image look pixelated when printed at a low resolution.

Above: Bitmap files can lose their quality when they are resized, unlike vectors, which can be scaled to any size without losing data. Bitmap files are larger but work better with raster images (pixels), and vectors are used for fonts and lines.

- **EPS (Encapsulated PostScript):** PostScript is a graphics description language used for communication between print devices and design programs. EPS preserves the quality of vectors and fonts and leaves any raster data intact. It's a portable format and can be opened and embedded in other applications, but it's not always editable.

- **AI (Adobe Illustrator):** This is the format used in an Illustrator file, which is a vector-based program. It's a limited and simplified subset of an EPS file. It has a decreased file size and is fully editable in Illustrator as it is the native file format.

- **TIFF (Tagged Image File Format):** This raster format contains a lot of image data and tends to be large. TIFF output is often used for high-resolution printing because quality isn't compromised, even when the file is compressed.

- **PDF (Adobe Portable Document Format):** PDF is a universal standard for transferring documents with a high-quality output because it preserves all the source data (fonts, vectors, images, colour) and can be opened, viewed and edited on any operating system. It can be exported from any graphics program, but remember to retain the print resolution at 300 dpi for high-quality jobs.

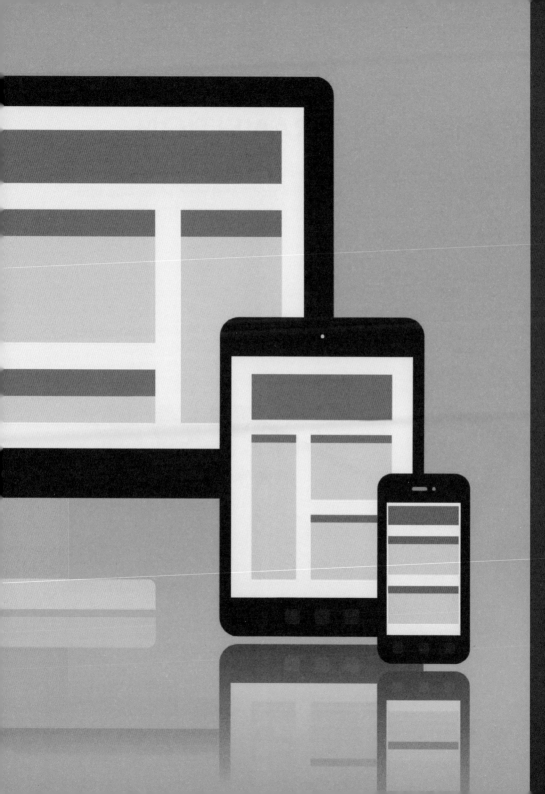

DESIGNING FOR SCREEN

MAKING THE TRANSITION

Designing for screen can be a hard transition for many designers to make, especially those who have been taught the traditional ways of working. With the insight this chapter provides, you will improve your workflow and learn some tips along the way.

FUNDAMENTAL PRINCIPLES

Although many of the design principles are the same, there are many new concepts to consider when producing work digitally. These are often overlooked, but with experience and patience, they can be learned and applied to every digital project you work on.

Below: These design principles apply in any digital project you work on.

Breaking the Rules

Whether you're an experienced designer, a student learning the basics or just looking to refresh your memory and learn some new techniques, this guide is for you. Rules are made to be broken, and different types of design work differently. Exploring everything from software to screen size, colour to coding, and typography to trends, here's how to become a more confident designer.

Below: Everyone is different and has their own way of working – it's about picking up small tricks and tips along the way.

SOFTWARE

The number of software packages available for designers can seem a little overwhelming, so we've picked out the most widely used ones to help you choose a package that will meet your needs.

PAID-FOR SOFTWARE

The following software is most commonly found in design studios, because the packages come with a hefty price tag. However, as with most things in life, you get what you pay for.

Adobe

Adobe Creative Cloud is the go-to software for the majority of designers, and offers a fantastic all-round package. Its vast Creative Suite has something for everyone, from junior designers to front-end developers. Every design, advertising and marketing agency uses Adobe software.

Adobe® Creative Cloud™

Above: Adobe Creative Cloud is the software of choice for most designers and illustrators.

- **Used By:** Creatives, from illustrators to developers.

- **Best Bits:** New features and frequent updates, integration of cloud storage, the whole suite of programs can be downloaded and installed, and settings can be synched to the cloud and accessed across machines.

- **Top Tip:** Adobe has stopped selling the software as separate products, with CDs to install and a manual – you now purchase it via a monthly subscription.

Adobe Photoshop

- ◉ **Used By**: Art-workers, retouchers, web designers and illustrators.

- ◉ **Best Bits**: The new addition allowing the space outside of the artboard to be used; fantastic pattern library, containing various elements.

- ◉ **Top Tip**: Try linking to images or other .psd documents to keep file size down.

Adobe Illustrator

- ◉ **Used By**: Illustrators, packaging designers and iconographers.

- ◉ **Best Bits**: The ability to set the corner radius (rounded corners), which scales up and down as you resize elements.

- ◉ **Top Tip**: Struggling with colour combinations? Try the Window/ Colour Guide, where you can select some suggested colour harmonies.

Above: Photoshop is the go-to app for many design tasks. It's flexible and powerful enough for image retouching and manipulation.

Above: The perfect program for many character designers and vector artists. Flexible, editable and easily applied to various projects.

Adobe InDesign

- **Used By**: Art-workers, print and layout designers.

- **Best Bits**: Typekit integration, Adobe libraries and device preview.

- **Top Tip**: Store graphic elements you've created, such as text frames or groups of objects, in Creative Cloud Library – perfect for quick access to all your assets from one place.

Above: Used for the majority of print-based design tasks, InDesign also handles presentations and PDF creation with ease.

Above: Agency life is fast-paced and relentless, so designers need software that can handle the demand.

FREE SOFTWARE

Not everyone has the money to spend on high-end software. Fortunately, there is plenty of free design software out there to kick-start your creative career.

InkScape

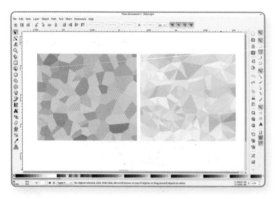

Above: InkScape is a free, open-source vector graphics editor. Great for those on a budget or just starting out.

Sketch

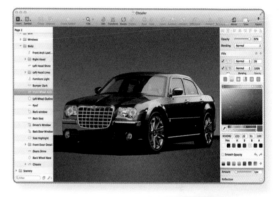

Above: Sketch gives you the power, flexibility and speed you always wanted in a lightweight and easy-to-use package.

GIMP

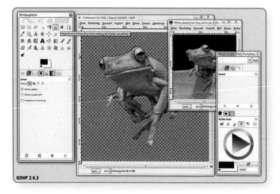

Above: GIMP is a free, open-source, cross-platform image editor available for GNU/Linux, OS X and Windows.

Blender

Above: Blender is a professional, free, open-source 3D computer graphics software program, used to create 3D elements and visual effects.

ONLINE APPLICATIONS

As the way we view pages online and our browsing habits have changed, so has the way we present designs to clients. If you're designing an app, for example, showing the designs within the mobile phone can help to sell the idea and see how elements display. There are some great online applications out there to help with this.

Marvel

Above: Marvel is the easiest way to turn your sketches, images and mock-ups into realistic mobile and web prototypes.

InVision

Above: Upload your design files and add animations, gestures and transitions to easily transform your static screens into clickable, interactive prototypes online.

UXPin

Redesigning the way w

Above: UXPin enables product teams and designers to build low- and high-fidelity, interactive, realistic web and mobile wireframes and prototypes.

SCREEN SIZES

There was a time when designing for the web was much simpler. Monitor resolutions were set in stone, and websites, online brochures and everything else were designed to fit that size. Now we have to consider multiple devices, each with different resolutions, with new devices being developed almost every day.

RESPONSIVE DESIGN

One difficult transition for print designers is to learn that web pages can be fluid in their layout, rearranging responsively to fit the browser window. Responsive web design ensures that a web page looks great no matter what size it is viewed at, whether on an iMac or a smartphone. How

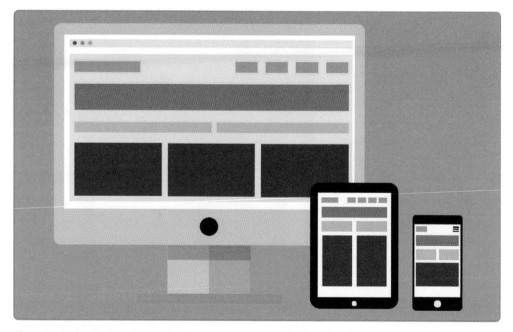

Above: Understanding how elements 'stack' and display on various devices is key when designing a website.

Above: Today's mobile phones and tablets are the go-to devices for getting in contact and browsing the web.

Right: It's not a simple task to create designs that look beautiful across so many different devices, with new ones being developed each week.

many times have you visited a site on your phone and had to pinch to zoom in, scrolling horizontally just to find what you are looking for?

MOBILE FIRST

Responsive web design has shifted how we design and build websites. Many designers now use best practice and design for mobile first. Mobile browsing

has now overtaken desktop, because more of us use our smartphone or tablet as our primary device. This means it is vital that the information is clear, concise and presented in a way in which the reader can understand it.

MOVING THE GOAL POSTS

Responsive web design is not only about adjusting to screen resolutions and scaling images and text to fit, but it's a whole new way of thinking about design. People now use five different devices on average, and consume more than 11 different sources of content online.

Is Touch the Future?

Touch-screen devices are becoming increasingly popular. Something that once only added functionality on smaller devices is now the input method of choice for larger, more powerful machines – the Microsoft Surface Pro and Apple iPad Pro, for example. Running as touch-screen tablets, they can be paired with a keyboard and mouse to transform into a laptop.

Below: Touch devices are becoming more powerful and capable of managing tasks previously only achieved on a desktop or laptop.

IMPACT OF LAYOUT

User experience (UX) is how a person feels when interacting with a system. This system can be a website, software or application. UX looks at factors such as ease of use, being able to find what you're after, and performing routine tasks. The idea is that design decisions are based on the needs and wants of the user, not just making something look good.

TAILOR TO YOUR AUDIENCE

Bear in mind that everyone is different. What works for one person might not work for another and vice versa. We can only lead a user down a path; we cannot force them to make decisions, or purchase a certain product.

Above: More and more websites are being created around the user experience and shopping patterns.

Accessibility

Accessibility is important. Not everyone has an up-to-date operating system or platform; some might have slower internet connections or older mobile devices. People might use screen readers or have the ability to adjust text size when browsing online.

Above: Everyone behaves differently, so there is no rule for the perfect shopping experience.

An Image Speaks a Thousand Words

Image size is still key within emails and websites. Eighty per cent of people give up on content because the images haven't loaded. Other reasons include the content being too long or unattractive. It's amazing how engagement increases massively on Twitter if you post a photo along with the tweet.

Quick Tip

Sometimes A/B testing is required to discover which design is more successful than others. It can be down to copy or image amends, and data gives a good indication of what's working.

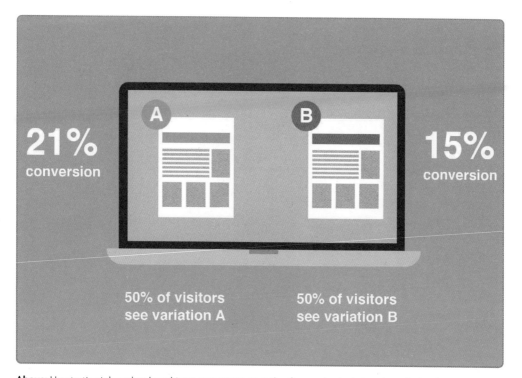

Above: User testing is key when launching a new service, to gather figures about what works and what does not.

ENHANCE YOUR DESIGN

This section includes a number of top tips to transform your design from being good to being great. Some may seem obvious, but are often overlooked by designers, no matter their age or experience.

UNDERSTAND THE PROJECT

It might sound obvious, but this is vital. You must understand the requirements of a website, for example. Always read the brief and flag up any issues before it's too late. An e-commerce site is functionally and visually very different from a portfolio or gallery page.

Above: Collaboration is key to understanding the design process and learning from other areas of design.

Web design
12 column grid ✓
Web fonts ✓
Max width 1140px ✓
Wireframe as a base ✓
Mobile first! ✓
Design call to actions ✓
H1, H2 & body copy ✓

SPEAK UP

Communicate with the client throughout the process. It's a good idea to set clear deadlines and ensure you have everything you need to fulfil the brief. Remember: it is a two-way process and working together helps to build an honest and upfront relationship. Ask other designers for help – bouncing ideas off each other is rewarding and worthwhile.

Left: Working to a process or specific method helps you achieve your goals.

TWO HEADS BETTER THAN ONE

If you're working on a website project, speak to a developer beforehand. Find out about any restrictions or limitations that might be in place. Knowing about the document setup size, use of a grid, web fonts, image sizes and the number of pages all help the process to be seamless and pain-free.

ORGANIZATION

Ensure that you work in an organized and productive manner. Creating a separate folder for assets can speed up the design and build process massively. This means you can create a toolkit of assets, which can simply be dragged and dropped into each new page or design.

Right: An example of organized layers within Photoshop (PS). Folders and colours can help you stay on top of clutter.

Above: The hamburger menu has become de rigueur
for most contemporary, sleek-looking websites.

HAMBURGER MENU

As the way we use the internet shifts, so do trends in web design – the 'hamburger' menu, for
example. The hamburger menu refers to the little three-lined button (see in the top-left corner
of the image here). It is a handy sidebar that frees up space within the design that otherwise
would have been taken up by clunky menus and drop-down lists. While it has faced criticism,
there's no doubt that its widespread use makes the function easily recognizable for users.

Above: Here is a great example of large, full-width images being used to add impact and impress the user.

COLOUR

Many print-based designers are aware of the potential pitfalls when sending a file to print – bleed, trapping, spread and so on – but for many digital-based designers, the world of colour can be a scary place. The first thing you should do is ensure that colour is standardized between various devices.

SCREEN TYPE

You will rarely be working on a brand new machine, especially when working in-house. Colours on a well-lit, new iMac on full brightness look a million miles away from how they render on a smaller 19-inch LCD display. Not everyone works with full brightness, for example – they might sit near a window or in a bright office with plenty of artificial light.

Above: Colour and contrast may appear vastly different depending on your computer setup.

CMYK   **RGB**

COLOUR MODES

Ensure you are working at the correct colour mode: RGB for screen, CMYK for print.

CALIBRATION

Calibrate your screen, scanner and other devices if possible. There are many professional-grade tools out there to help.

Above: The main colour breakdowns for print (cyan, magenta, yellow and black) and screen (red, green and blue).

Above: Calibrating your screen, scanner and printer ensures consistency across your devices.

Quick Tip

Disabling Photoshop's colour management for RGB documents forces RGB colours displayed on screen and exported to saved files to match the actual colour value.

Left: The latest hardware has brighter, more pixel-dense screens than ever before.

FINAL TWEAKS

There's a good chance that an iPhone, iPad or Apple Watch looks vastly different from your computer's display. The screen type and warmth/coolness of colour can vary greatly. This probably means that the colour breakdowns can be tweaked once you see the app, for example, in situ. This is especially true with higher-pixel-density monitors, such as Retina and 4K.

ADJUST THE CONTRAST

Contrast within colours can make or break a design. A text colour that is too similar to the background colour is very hard to read. Also, text with too much contrast can be difficult to discern. For example, white text on black is very unnatural and difficult to read.

Above: Ensuring there is enough contrast between your colours is key. There are many resources online that can help you.

ACCESSIBLE FOR ALL

In terms of accessibility and legibility, a ratio of 7:1 is preferred. There are many resources available to help you check contrast and colours. Think about large text as well as body copy.

Above: Some users require specialist software to help them read text on screen. Screen readers and other programs can help.

Colour Wheel

Finding colour schemes in your work can be difficult, but there are many tricks to make it easier. Remember the colour wheel you used in school? Now is the perfect time to revisit it. Colour harmony is critical in design work.

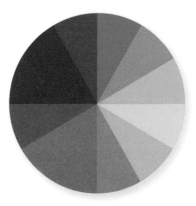

Right: The classic colour wheel. This can help with colour selection, applying rules and discovering new colour schemes.

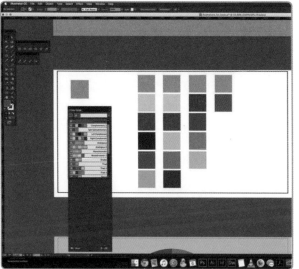

Above: Using some features of Illustrator, you can formulate great colour palettes for your designs.

Applying the Rules

There are some formulas that guarantee a harmonious outcome, such as analogous colours. These are three colours that are side by side on the colour wheel. Complementary colours are two that are directly opposite each other on the colour wheel, such as red and green, or yellow and purple. These opposing colours create maximum contrast and stability for your work. Finally, think about colour context – how the colour appears in relation to other colours next to or around it.

Help from the Professionals

Adobe Color (previously Kuler) is great for finding interesting colour schemes and importing them into your software. You can share them with others and import them as swatches. There is even an app that colour picks from photographs and your camera. This is perfect when you're on the go and want to save interesting colour combinations.

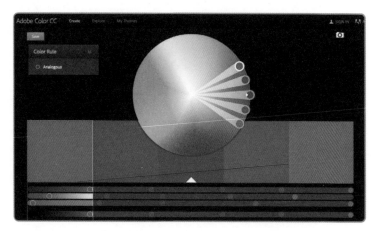

Above: Adobe Color is a fantastic website for inspiration. Swatches can be shared, downloaded and created at the touch of a button.

TYPOGRAPHY

Great typography is one of the most important aspects when it comes to turning a good project into an outstanding one. Covering colour, size, line length, type, spacing and much more, this section discusses the key factors for designing on screen. Good typography ensures the highest-quality end result.

BASICS FIRST

Always start with the basics: leading (line height), tracking (letter spacing), line length and kerning. Do not always rely on the computer to typeset the words perfectly. You need to master details such as clicking your type tool between two characters and using the Alt and arrow keys to adjust the kerning between them.

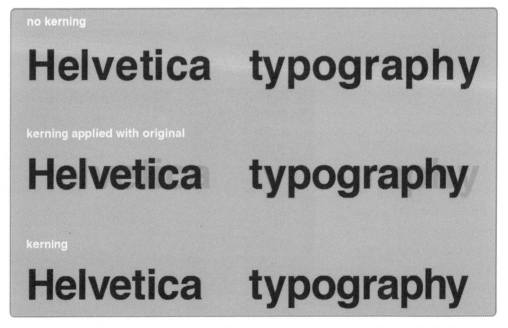

no kerning

Helvetica typography

kerning applied with original

Helvetica typography

kerning

Helvetica typography

Above: Kerning your letterforms is important and can really help take a project to the next level. A keen eye for detail is required.

Above: Play around with type combinations. See what works and helps reflect the brand's message.

GET THE BALANCE RIGHT

You have to choose a typeface that relates to your target audience and aligns with your message. We're not talking about designing your whole email in an obscure font, but headlines and subheads should be tailored to your target audience. Helvetica and Arial are great for body copy, but headlines can offer something more. Text must be clear and legible.

Above: Web fonts have revolutionized how designers use fonts – new fonts can be downloaded and added for use in your work in seconds.

WHAT ARE WEB FONTS?

One of the greatest improvements in web design in recent years is the ability to use web fonts. These are fonts that are hosted on sites such as Google Fonts, Fontdeck and Adobe Typekit, and available to use in your design. On the surface, web fonts and desktop fonts are very similar. However, a web font tends to have its glyphs and additional characters removed. This means that, as a designer, you do not have as much flexibility, but this can be refined with code during the build.

Advantages of Web Fonts

(1) They are compatible with all web browsers and are SEO-friendly.

(2) Using web fonts saves money, because you do not need to purchase font licences.

(3) They are incorporated into your design using a line of code.

(4) Fonts can be changed throughout a site at the touch of a button.

Above: The use of web fonts has made designing and building websites so much easier. A font can be changed throughout a 20-page site by changing a line of code. Simple and powerful.

Typographic Trends

Throughout 2015 and into 2016, we've seen numerous typographical trends emerging:

1. Extreme size, both large and small, to add emphasis.

2. Text superimposed over images.

3. Hand-drawn and decorative type, and artistic fonts.

Quick Tip

With the right typography, text becomes an artistic element as well as content. Allow a well-designed font to grab the reader's attention. When combined with negative space, large images and a well-thought-out colour scheme, it can really make your design stand out. Experiment and do not be scared to make mistakes.

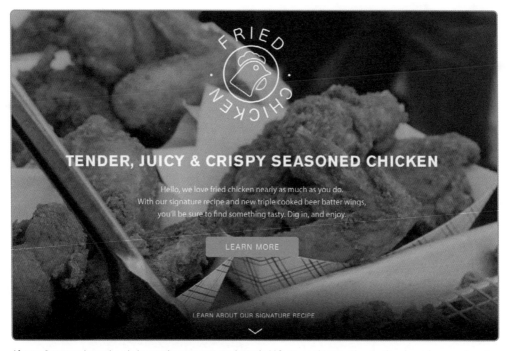

Above: Current web trends include using large images, overlaying bold fonts, combining with a simple colour scheme, and much more.

RESOLUTION

Image resolution is a minefield and a tricky concept to get your head around, especially for new designers. The first thing you need to know is that there are two types of images when designing for screen: vector and bitmap.

Above: Vectors are a series of paths or points that create individual shapes – the building blocks of creating vector artwork.

WHAT ARE VECTORS?

Vectors are easier to understand. Created in software, such as Adobe Illustrator, vector graphics are a series of points that build up shapes, and each object can be edited separately. For example, the colour, shape, size and position can be adjusted easily. Files such as EPS, AI and SVG are mathematical – they can be scaled infinitely. This means that when you resize them, they do not lose quality.

WHAT ARE BITMAPS?

Bitmap images – such as JPG, GIF, PNG and PSD – are made up of individual pixels or dots. Unlike vectors, when pixels are resized, they lose quality.

Right: Here you can see the differences between vector- and bitmap-based images.

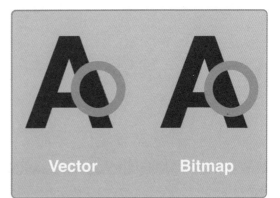

Vector   Bitmap

DPI AND PPI

DPI, or dpi, stands for 'dots per inch'. The higher the DPI, the more information there is within an image; the more dots, the crisper the image appears on screen. Although DPI is a print term, it is transferable to digital design. PPI, or ppi, stands for 'pixels per inch', and refers to on-screen work.

Above: Ensure that you are selecting the correct colour mode, depending on your output. Print-ready images might display differently on screen.

WEB IMAGES

All images display at 72 dpi online. Your image could contain more information and actually be 300 dpi, but 72 dpi is as much as you can usefully reproduce on screen. This means that if you have a 300 dpi image, it won't look any better than a 72 dpi one on screen.

Below: All images display on screen at 72 dpi, no matter how many pixels the image might contain.

Quick Tip

Due to technical advances, faster internet connections and data compression, we're now seeing more image-heavy websites. A current trend is to have a large 'hero' image above the fold or scroll. Because our sense of vision is so strong, using a large image is one of the fastest ways to grab a user's attention.

Above: There are ways to scale up JPG images without losing any quality.

THE IMAGE JIGSAW

Interpolation is typically used to scale an image up to a larger size, using an algorithm to automatically fill in pixels where there is missing information to complete the image. In other words, it tries to guess how it should fill in a pixel based on the pixels around it.

Above: Current trends include using short videos as hero images, mainly thanks to faster internet connections.

TIPS FOR BETTER WEB DESIGN

The next few pages contain a few top tips and hints for you when you are planning your next design project. Experiment using the advice we have already given you, but best of all, enjoy experimenting and making your own rules!

MULTIPLE TYPEFACES?

Traditionally, it is recommended not to use more than two typefaces on a website design. Too many can create conflict and can lead to a confused and cluttered site, with no real hierarchy. Remember that legibility and readability are key. If the viewer cannot find what they are after, you have overworked the design. Rules are meant to be broken though, and there's nothing to say that more than two typefaces cannot work together to good effect. Experiment and see what works for you.

SET SOME RULES

Too many type sizes and styles together can wreck any layout. A typographic scale has a limited set of type sizes that work well together, along with a layout grid – such as 12, 14, 18, 24, 30 and 36 pt. It's important to have a clear hierarchy between the header, subhead, caption, body copy, pull quote and so on.

Right: Bootstrap is a great resource for creating and designing digital content. Strict rules and clear instructions make it easier.

Typography

Headings

All HTML headings, `<h1>` through `<h6>`, are available. `.h1` through `.h6` classes are also available, for when you want to match the font styling of a heading but still want your text to be displayed inline.

EXAMPLE

h1. Bootstrap heading
Semibold 36px

h2. Bootstrap heading
Semibold 30px

h3. Bootstrap heading
Semibold 24px

h4. Bootstrap heading
Semibold 18px

h5. Bootstrap heading
Semibold 14px

h6. Bootstrap heading
Semibold 12px

```
<h1>h1. Bootstrap heading</h1>
<h2>h2. Bootstrap heading</h2>
<h3>h3. Bootstrap heading</h3>
<h4>h4. Bootstrap heading</h4>
<h5>h5. Bootstrap heading</h5>
<h6>h6. Bootstrap heading</h6>
```
Copy

Create lighter, secondary text in any heading with a generic `<small>` tag or the `.small` class.

EXAMPLE

h1. Bootstrap heading Secondary text

Overview
Grid system
Typography
  Headings
  Body copy
  Inline text elements
  Alignment classes
  Transformation classes
  Abbreviations
  Addresses
  Blockquotes
  Lists
Code
Tables
Forms
Buttons
Images
Helper classes
Responsive utilities
Using Less
Using Sass

Back to top
Preview theme

THE PERFECT LINE LENGTH

Line length is important when you want to give the user a good reading experience. The right number of characters on each line is key to readability. If your line length is too long, the user will have a hard time focusing on the text, because the eye finds it difficult to make out where the line starts and ends. Around 50 to 60 characters per line is deemed the optimal line length.

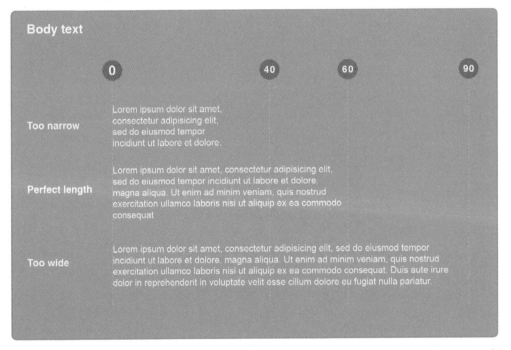

Above: Line length is key for a good reading experience: 50–60 characters per line is perfect and encourages the user to read.

FONT SELECTION

Experiment with fonts – a mixture of serif and sans serif, for example. Aim for clean and clear presentation, which also reflects the brand's visual style. Many designers prefer to make their headlines sans serif, to give them more appeal, because sans serif fonts are easy to read and look good. Serif fonts are seen as traditional, with an air of formality, while sans serif fonts feel reliable.

Comic Sans

Times New Roman

Courier

LIVE TEXT

The use of 'live text' in emails has become easier and more common. Live text is overlaying HTML text over an image. With the introduction of web fonts, a designer can tie into the brand look and feel by using the same fonts used across the brand. Subscribers have the option to read emails with images turned off, so by using live text, they won't miss anything important, compared to supplying the graphic with text flattened in Photoshop, for example.

Above: Live text and alt tags in emails help the user to understand the content, even with images turned off.

WORKING WITH OTHERS

COLLABORATION

You now have the necessary know-how to be able to produce high-quality, smart and legible designs in ways that will attract attention and convey a purposeful and organized message. However, being a designer is never a solitary job. There are many people a designer has to liaise with throughout every job. This chapter concentrates on issues related to being a working designer.

BEING A WORKING DESIGNER

A good designer should always gather and ask for as much information as possible prior to starting the actual work and layout of the design. This is essentially what being a graphic and digital designer is all about, otherwise there is the risk of treading the murky waters between design and art, where authorship means renouncing the limitations and perspectives imposed by others.

Below: As the designer, you are constantly liaising with different contributing people.

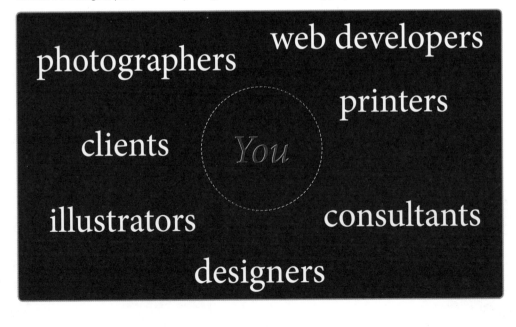

Compromise

When working for other people, there has to be balance and compromise between the client's concept and a designer's expertise, and how they can translate said concept into a clear visual and typographic language.

Restrictions

Clients are not the only ones influencing and dictating the design process. The prospective end result will be a combination of the work and ideas of clients, printers, illustrators, photographers, web developers and other designers. In addition to the fluctuating number of people, other factors affecting each design job are the budget and the target market. Who will the readers be? Can it be printed on uncoated 150 gsm cream paper with gold foil, without worrying about the cost? How much custom code and third-party integrations need to be added to a website without going over the budget? The designer needs to form layouts and work with each of these constraints.

Above: The designer's job is to be a graphic translator, so that the audience can appreciate the client's original idea in a tangible way.

Constraints

You will also experience constraints as a result of the type of work you undertake and designer you choose to be. As a freelance designer, you can choose your jobs and the amount you want to manage. You may have fewer restrictions: you can ultimately decide what the design is going to be like, but this comes with added responsibility, such as running your own client service. Working for an agency or company usually means adhering to brand guidelines and restrictions, such as only working with certain colours, formats, fonts or materials. There are more people to liaise with and more approval stages because of this. However, there are other people (account managers) who supervise client services and sales, leaving the designer with more time to actually design.

TAKING A BRIEF

Each design job is unique and every client is different, so suffice to say that briefs vary from project to project. When taking a brief, it pays to get as much information as possible at an early stage to avoid confusion and misunderstandings further down the line.

DIFFERENT CLIENTS

Some clients have more experience and are more knowledgeable –they might be printers or designers themselves – so their briefs would probably cover the whole process from start to finish. On the other hand, other clients might be undertaking a design project for the first time. It is important to guide them along and ask them everything, in case they hadn't even thought about it themselves.

Clarify

When you receive a brief, make sure that anything you might need to know is included and that all the details are understood. Do not be afraid to chase the client for clearer information. Even if it seems obvious, it is better to get everything formalized from the very beginning.

OXFORD
UNIVERSITY PRESS

Cover Design Brief

INSTRUCTIONS:

- Read through the brief and prepare a jacket proof (front, back, spine and flaps—*see next page for guidance*) to the dimensions specified, using the copy provided, supplied separately as a Word doc.
- You should design 2 different cover options:
  1. An abstract design (image based)
  2. A purely typographic design
  Feel free to design a range of options, but we would like you to present 1 abstract & 1 typographic solution which should be displayed as front panels only (159 x 240mm). From these 2 cover designs please choose your favoured & design the complete jacket artwork.
  (*You do not need to make any purchases, watermarked images are fine.*)
- OXFORD should appear on front, back and spine somewhere. Do not be too concerned about accuracy of font/placement for the OXFORD logo, just ensure it is placed somewhere.
- Please place the barcode on the back panel, use at 100%.
- Bring along a colour print-out with your name clearly marked, no need for it to be high quality proof, a colour laser print-out will suffice. The print out should be at 100%.
  A pdf should also be submitted via email to HR at least 24 hours prior to the interview.
- Be prepared to discuss your designs with respect to the brief at interview.

Cover briefing form

Format/trimmed page size: 240 x 159 mm (portrait)   **Spine width:** 26mm

- Is it a purely typographical, abstract, or image based?   Abstract Image & typographic options required
- Any restraints on cropping or sizing the image?   No cropping restraints to any of the images
- How many colours can the designer use?   4 or 5
- Supplementary information about this book:

The hormone testosterone underlies the organization of activation of masculinity: it changes the body and brain to make a male. It is involved not only in sexuality but in driving aggression, competitiveness, risk-taking - all elements that were needed for successful survival and reproduction in the past. But these ancient systems are carried forward into a modern world. The ancient world shaped the human brain, but the modern world is shaped by that brain.

In *Testosterone*, Joe Herbert explains the nature of this potent hormone, how it operates in mammals in general and in humans in particular, what we know about its role in influencing various aspects of behaviour in men, and what we are beginning to understand of its role in women. From rape to gang warfare among youths, understanding the workings of testosterone is critical to enable us to manage its continuing powerful effects in modern society.

Readership: For popular science readers & undergraduate students studying biology & the life sciences.

Importance of the individual elements:	BIG	MEDIUM	SMALL
Title	☑	☐	☐
Sub-title	☐	☑	☐
Author(s)	☐	☑	☐

Above: This example of a design brief from a publishing house includes what the job is about, what it's for and technical specs such as format, spine width and elements.

Help the Client

Occasionally, a prospective client might approach a designer, asking for something without exactly knowing how their message can be broadcast, thinking that a flyer will suit their needs when in reality it would be a website or vice versa. You must ask the right questions to point the client in the right direction, even if that sometimes means sending a job away because they need an industrial designer instead of a graphic designer. This is when an extensive and well-thought-out brief can save the day.

Here are some ideal questions to ask when a client is indecisive:

1. What do you want to show in the design (print or online) and how do you want it to be perceived?
2. Who is your target audience?
3. What is the agency/company/client like and what is their identity?
4. What kind of deliverables are you expecting?
5. Are there any examples you want to base the design on?
6. What/who is your competition? What is the budget?

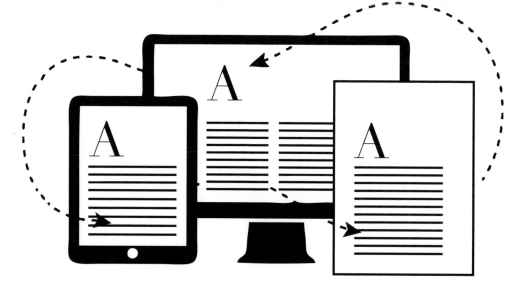

Above: By asking the right questions, you can find out whether the design would benefit from being online instead of printed, or both.

The Comprehensive Brief

A good brief should have all the obvious and technical information, as well as the more subjective, intangible aspects. Apart from knowing whether the design will be accessed online or in print, the designer should know the materials that will be used. It is important to know if it will be seen on digital devices or on a specific type of paper. The following list should help make sure the brief is comprehensive enough to avoid any unnecessary headaches.

(1) **What is the job?** Is it a logo, a web design or some campaign branding? Whatever the project, it is essential to know what will be necessary for the job: It is necessary to ask if

Below: This is another example of starting to design a layout, with dimensions, font styles, colours and elements.

the client has existing templates or brand guidelines that they want you to follow. Find out how they will supply the material and in what file types (PDF, Word documents, TIFF, JPEG). Check if they use a specific palette of colours or/and fonts.

(2) **In-house or outsource?** Depending on the images, you might need a photographer, stock photos or to create the images yourself. If it's a website, you might need a web developer or a printer. If it were a children's book, maybe a specific type of illustrator would be beneficial.

(3) **Target market?** Who will be reading the book or using the site? Find out the age range, gender and background of interests.

Left and Above: When researching the first stages of a design job, it is important to discover similar brands, materials and the competition.

④ **Competition**. The competition might be another company, brand, product or designer. Your client's design should offer something unique that the others don't. The design should attract attention and look different and interesting. Scouting the competition, researching and taking note of what other similar websites or book genres look like is a worthwhile exercise. There are certain elements that become entrenched into visual social conventions, such as particular fonts used for women's magazines or thinking that sans serif typefaces work better on screen and serifs are more legible for long-form print.

⑤ **Size, layout, type, structure**. It is important to know what the dimensions are, as well as the extent of the print run and the platform it will need. Ask how many deliverables the client will need and if the format will change. Knowing the size and the content of the design will make it easier to choose typefaces and image style, and to create the layout.

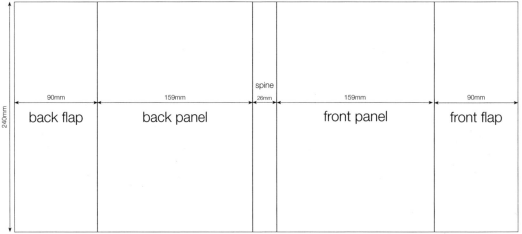

Above: This is another way to instruct a designer: showing a template of measurements and an actual grid and structure.

⑥ **Tech Specs**. The design should either be in CMYK or RGB, depending on whether it will be printed or browsed online. The tech specs will also depend on the program it will be created in:

InDesign, Photoshop or Illustrator. Remember what the best file type for exporting is and don't forget the proper resolution.

Right: You should confirm what type of design is needed (digital or print) before starting to consider colour, resolution, size and so on.

Below: This is an example of a layout, specifying margins, fonts, spaces and grids.

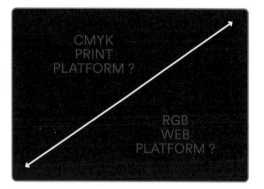

CMYK
PRINT
PLATFORM ?

RGB
WEB
PLATFORM ?

15mm	144.6mm	7.3mm	12.7mm	12.7mm	7.3mm	144.6mm	15mm	Grid

100% scale

16.9mm

38.1mm

KNIGHT
Who are you?

DEATH
I am Death.

KNIGHT
Have you come for me?

DEATH
I have been walking by
your side for a long time.

KNIGHT
That I know.

190.5mm

DEATH
Are you prepared?

KNIGHT
My body is frightened,
but I am not.

Optima
9.5pt/12pt
with an
extension
of 200%
always in
gray Pantone
7544C

DEATH
Well, there is no shame
in that.

228.6mm

The knight has risen
to his feet. He shivers.
Death opens his cloak
to place it around the
knight's shoulders.

139.7mm

Caslon 540
Roman
9.3pt/12pt
Always ragged
when in
dialogue

KNIGHT
Wait a moment.

DEATH
That's what they all say.
I grant no reprieves.

KNIGHT
You play chess, don't you?

12.7mm

4.2mm

9

16.3mm

Caslon 540
Regular 7pts
Only on the
right page

150mm

150mm

Above: Define dates for approvals and different deadlines.

⑦ **Deadlines.** It is important to talk about dates, schedules and deadlines at this stage. Ask when the dates for each approval stage should be and what the deadline is for the final files to be sent to the printer or uploaded online. This is the best way to organize the workflow.

⑧ **Budget and fees.** Finally, a budget and a price need to be defined once a designer understands the full extent of the project. Sometimes a client will have a limited budget and this will outline the full scope of the project. This should include costs for copywriting, illustrations or web development. The client should budget the printing and material costs separately. Lastly, the fee should be a reflection of the amount of work that will be put into the design.

Above: The budget can determine the design. This silver cloth-bound book with spot ink screen-printed on to the cover and a red-sprayed edge would require a higher budget.

BALANCING ACT

Part of being a designer is being able to balance what someone else wants with the freedom to freely express a creative side. Delivering a great design is the juxtaposition of a designer's expertise and inventiveness with a client's needs and strong ideas. A designer can fight hard for their designs, but at the end of the day the client is paying and has the final say.

UNDERTAKING THE DESIGN

There are still some stages in the design process to watch out for, even once all the necessary organization is out of the way and the actual design begins. It is customary to start with an assortment of diverse options and to go through approval phases and have some changes made throughout.

CRITICISM IS NECESSARY

Part of the job description is receiving criticism. Design is a subjective discipline and has no clear-cut rules, only guidelines. It is extremely likely that many clients won't have the same design education, background and experience as you, so it is critical to have a professional – and preferably positive – perspective on criticism. It may not be agreeable, but it can call attention to mistakes and knowing how to use it effectively can be a designer's biggest asset.

Use Feedback

Honest feedback can help a designer grow and even motivate them. When accepting any project, go into it with an open mind and a helpful attitude, and remember that not everyone will agree, and they will have different tastes and opinions. By first understanding the criticism, and where the client is coming from, it becomes easier to use it to your advantage and consequently respond in a reasonable and helpful way. Here are a few tips and tricks when dealing with criticism:

- **Expectations**: Align your expectations with that of the client and be open to different views.

Above: Align your expectations with the client's to avoid misunderstandings and frustrations.

● **Remove yourself from the equation:** Do not take criticism personally. It is constructive feedback on the work, not on you. Be mindful of this.

{ Client

criticism

you }

{ Client

criticism

design }

Above: Do not take criticism personally, and try to guide the client into giving precise and constructive feedback.

● **Use it or lose it:** Try to see it from the client's perspective. Sometimes we develop habits we do not notice, and criticism can focus on blind spots and help improve your own design standards.

● **Communication:** If the criticism is vague, ask for specifics. Some comments may be too subjective and useless with no real substance – 'This is not what I want,' or, 'This is ugly.' This gross misunderstanding should have been avoided with a detailed brief, but in this case, the client might not have explained things clearly or expected something different. Guide the criticism into something more objective and defined.

● **Learning:** Some criticism might take you down a path where a new skill or technique is required to finish or improve the design.

● **Stay grounded:** Respect the client (and yourself), and learn from every criticism and situation.

Approval Stages

Some clients might not be very experienced or have difficulty making up their minds, so the number of approvals can get out of hand. These should be kept to a minimum, otherwise the process might get too chaotic and cause problems. If it passes the point where all the extra changes (and work) cause you to start losing money and wasting too much time, there is always the unfortunate option of giving an ultimatum or walking away. To avoid this, make sure there is good communication from the beginning, and agree to a specific (or approximate) number of stages for the project. Two to three rounds of amends is reasonable before starting to charge extra.

Above: Remember that showing annotations, grids, colour palettes and the overall framework can help the client understand the design process and the work going into the final design result.

Range of Solutions

There is always more than one way to reach a visual solution for any project. There is no right or wrong way to design anything, so it is always acceptable and practical to create more than one option when showing a client. Too much choice can be time-consuming, confusing and lead to indecisiveness, but a minimum of three design alternatives is good practice. Avoid designing the same idea with only slight changes.

The range of alternatives has to be completely different and have different routes. Annotations in the design can help the client understand the process and what the final result can be, as it is not always possible to talk them through it directly.

Below: Try to show a minimum of three different design solutions, but do not go overboard. This book cover example is showing two sets of three book jackets to work in a series.

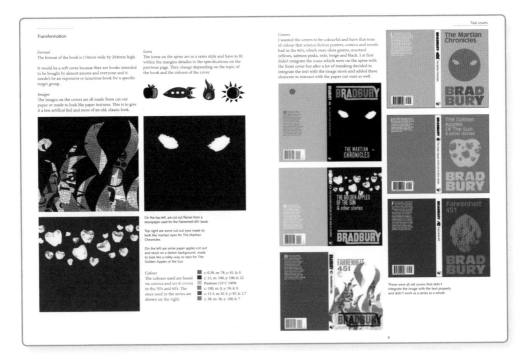

Above: This is the final solution for a book cover series project, showing three approved jackets.

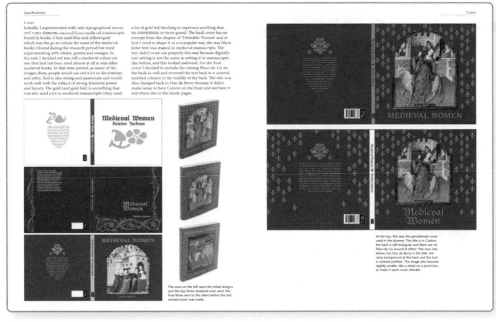

Above: This example shows the three design options on the left, and the final solution on the right.

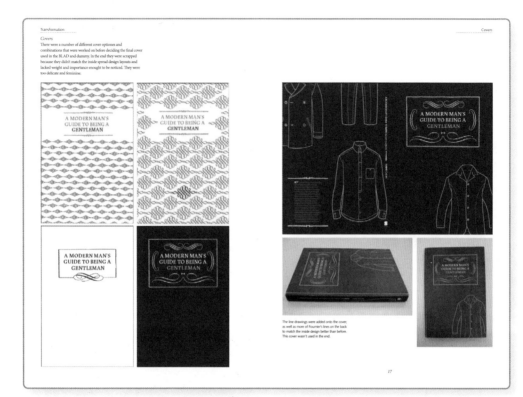

Above: The four covers on the left are different design alternatives, and the cover on the right is the final product.

Hitting the Deadline

The best advice for this is to set reasonable and realistic expectations. Schedule due dates and be clear about all the levels and revisions, and when the client can expect to see results. Stay in regular contact and keep them updated throughout the process. Finally, remember to break down each stage into logical time slots for yourself — and make it feasible. More often than not, the job takes longer than expected. It's better to finish early than to miss a deadline.

Images

For the images, I think it is important to emphasise that I wanted to apply the same kind of reverence to the images as was given to the text. This was done by using the woodcuts by Thomas Bewick in exactly the same size, without having to subvert them by enlarging them or changing them in any way. These were scanned from the book *Thomas Bewick Vignettes*, by Iain Bain (printed in 1978). All of the images are very small and delicate: a feature of Thomas Bewick's woodcuts. I kept the feather on the front cover, found on page 76 of said book, exactly the same size as the original woodcut: 56.5mm high by 20.8mm wide. If I was treating the poems in such a way, I would also not touch the original image in any way. The only problem was getting the printer to translate the high resolution scanned image onto paper but it seemed it wasn't able to reproduce the exact same meticulous lines that are palpable in woodcuts.

I wanted the other images to be treated in the same way (being the original size) but because the format of the poetry books are so small, the images wouldn't be seen properly or appreciated and the cover series might look too different from each other. Therefore I decided to keep the Thomas Bewick woodcuts to its original size and just make the other images proportional in size and fit on the format.

The woman with the tentacle legs is from the contemporary artist Dan Hillier and her original size is 480mm high by 330mm wide. The artist makes "altered engravings" where he seems to add and mix an image with another (in this case, the woman with the tentacles).

The woodcuts from the third book are from Bryan Nash Gill, another contemporary artist that cuts wood and prints directly from them. That is why his prints are extremely large because they're actual tree-sized woodcuts. The woodcut I used on the cover is 857mm wide by 635mm high. The woodcut is Cedar Burl, also known as Alaskan Yellow, wood that comes from Cypress trees.

Woodcut feather
by Thomas Bewick.
56.5mm x 20.8mm

Woodcut feathers
by Thomas
Bewick, same area
size as original
feather in the
poetry books.

Altered engravings
by Dan Hillier.
330mm x 480mm

Woodcuts by
Bryan Nash Gill.
From bottom to
top. Crescent 1/1
1003mm x 635mm;
Willow 1/10
1260mm x 981mm;
Cedar Burl 1/15
857mm

Above: There are many ways to reach a solution in any design, but it is unnecessary to spend too much time researching or finding too many options if deadlines are tight.

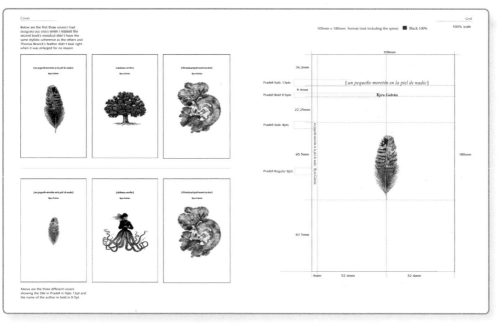

Cover　　　　　　　　　　　　　　　　　　　　　　　　　　　　　　　　　　　　　*Grid*

Below are the first three covers I had designed but that's when I realised the second book's woodcut didn't have the same stylistic coherence as the others and Thomas Bewick's feather didn't look right when it was enlarged for no reason.

105mm x 185mm format (not including the spine)　■ Black 100%　100% scale

Above are the three different covers showing the title in Pradell Italic 13pt and the name of the author in bold in 9.5pt.

109mm

26.3mm

Pradell Italic 13pts　　{ un pequeño moretón en la piel de nadie }
Pradell Bold 9.5pts　　Kyra Galván
9.4mm

22.25mm

Pradell Italic 8pts

65.5mm　　　　　　　　　　　　　　　　　　　　185mm

Pradell Regular 8pts

61.5mm

4mm　　52.4mm　　52.4mm

Above: Sometimes you will find you reach a decision without any extra options or alternatives. This is fine but the design has to be carefully refined and approved.

DELIVERING THE FINAL JOB

So the design job is finished and approved, but the work still isn't done. This might be the most delicate part of the process, because it requires a high level of attention to detail and making sure all that hard work does not go to waste by messing up the files. The final product needs to be delivered appropriately.

THE MEANS TO FINISH THE JOB

At this final stage, the project should have been designed in the correct colour mode, in the appropriate program, and saved and exported with the required file format. Images and fonts should have been checked for licences and copyrights. Make sure nothing is missing and that the files are print-ready, or that the web hosting is working and has been paid for.

Below:
Test your fonts and make sure they work and can be exported correctly. Do not forget to acquire licences for them if needed.

ANTIQUE OLIVE SÉRIE COMPACT

ABCDEFGHIJK
LMNOPQR
STUVWXYZ

&ÇÆŒÈÉÊË-?!0":';,.

abcdefghijk
lmnopqr
stuvwxyz

çæœèàâêèéèèëïîöòùûü

1234567890

Antique Olive

This humanist sans serif, like Gill Sans, was actually designed in the 60's by French typographer Roger Excoffon. Unlike Charcoal. this typeface has 8 different weights. Although perhaps not as geometric or straight as other sans serif's, Antique Olive has unique strokes and modulations that give it a lot of character and was just what I was looking for.

The Martian Chronicles
RAY BRADBURY

Franklin Gothic

Franklin Gothic was used for the back blurb of the books because although Antique Olive worked well as a big display kind of title for the covers, it would be too much to use in a lot more text. So, F. Gothic is a typical realist sans serif with a more traditional double-story g and a and worked well for the back, being also an older kind of typeface to use for the books.

Gill Sans

Gill Sans and its variations has been used in many futuristic things because of its geometricity, yet it lacks that old vibe from the 50's/60's with their wonky strokes and display type letterings.

The Martian Chronicles
RAY BRADBURY

Charcoal

Charcoal has that 60's vibe but it lacks variations in widths and visual options. It would also perhaps be too pastige yet not enough.

The Martian Chronicles
RAY BRADBURY

Copyrights and Trust

Unfortunately, some jobs can fall through and disappear, even after a lot of work has gone into them. This can happen for any number of reasons, and though it can be tempting to sue the client, this is only possible if there were properly signed contracts from the beginning, which is not always the case. There are ways to help prevent these problems, such as asking to be paid in instalments if the project is big; one part can be paid during the first proof stage and the last one for the final PDF delivery.

Watermarks

Another tip would be to watermark all the designs, so they cannot be used or edited until the final stage. In the end, you have to trust people, and if the worst comes to pass, the best solution would be to never work for that client again.

Below: When delivering files that are not yet ready, it would be advisable to watermark them. This protects them from misuse and they won't be confused with the final files.

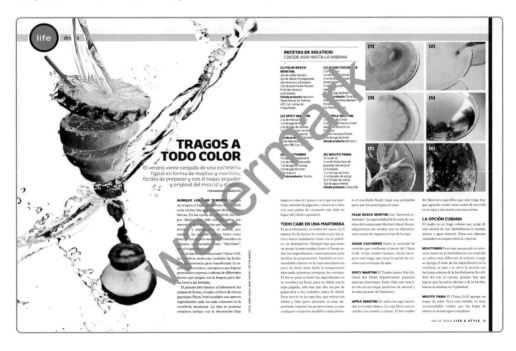

DO YOUR HOMEWORK

Supplying the right deliverables is a question of knowing how the files will be used. With print, any job can now be in a bespoke custom size, but only if the printers have certain capabilities. The printer has to be tailored to the job. Do your homework and find out about their products, sizing information and file requirements. There are many types and styles of printers – some more expensive than others – and while some may easily print high-quality, specialist jobs on heavy stock paper, others can work better with longer runs but cheaper ink or paper.

Above: With print, any job can be cut into a custom size. Each printer has certain capabilities, so check beforehand what is available to you.

Exporting and Packaging

Always supply the final, corrected and approved files in the right resolution and colours in one labelled package. Include fonts, links and even specification instructions for the printers or any future designers who could be modifying it later on. Everything should be clear, in sensibly

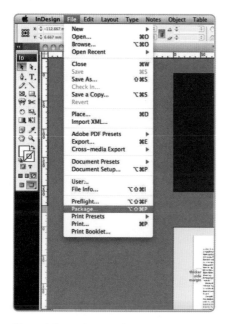

named folders, and all files should be backed up in case they get lost or corrupted. For large print jobs, InDesign has a handy Preflight feature that brings up any issues that could pose a problem when printing. Use the Package option in InDesign to automatically collect all the used fonts, links and files into one folder. The newer versions of Photoshop and Illustrator also have a feature that allows you to package fonts and links.

Above: InDesign has a useful option for packaging a job, which puts all the fonts, links and documents into one folder.

THE FULL STEP-BY-STEP

A brief summary of the complete process can help illustrate the workflow that goes into any design job. The following steps are meant for guidance and to help form a clearer understanding of the mechanisms when embarking on a project from start to finish.

(1) The first step always starts with the brief, then the research and the strategy. All the available information relevant to the job has to be collected at this stage. This includes finding out about existing branding to compare. All the people involved in the process and the materials that will be used need to be confirmed. This step is also for getting quotes and discussing prices and fees. Expectations and deadlines need to be outlined as well. Remember: what is its aim and whom is it meant to reach?

Right: Collect all the relevant information and research similar products and brands. This is a discovery and strategy stage.

② Once initial proposals and details have been accepted, the creative process can begin. The design can start to form, taking into account all the constraints established in the first stage. This is when the medium is settled and the designer can start choosing fonts, colour palettes, element styles, illustrations or photographs. Layout and space is defined. This is when three or more graphic solutions should be sent for the first approval stage. Receive feedback and criticism and decide on one preferred concept to be developed further.

Chapter Title Miller Roman 10pts, space above 90pts, below 10pts

Chapter Subtitle Miller italic 9pts, space below 13.5pts

The First Line Indent at the start of every paragraph text is in the regular Miller Display typeface and is of 13.5pts. The First Line Indent at the start of every paragraph text is in the regular Miller Display typeface and is of 13.5pts.

Collations are never indented and use **bold** and *italic*. They're in Miller Text Regular 6.5pts with a leading of 9.75pts. The space between normal text and collations is of 13.5pts. They will be before the footnotes

1 Option 2 for footnotes is being in two columns with a gutter space of 13.5pts.
2 The minimum space before first footnote is 18.5pts. Footnotes have a left tab of 10pts. These don't have a ruler.
3 They may also have *italic text* and are 7pts with 10.75pts.
4 Footnotes are Miller Display Regular 7pt with 10.75pts leading
5 Footnotes are Miller Display Regular 7pt with 10.75pts leading
6 The minimum space before first footnote is 18.5pts. Footnotes have a left tab of 10pts They may also have *italic text* and are 7pts with 10.75pts.
7 Footnotes are Miller Display Regular 7pt with 10.75pts leading

8 The minimum space before first footnote is 18.5pts. Footnotes have a left tab of 10pts They may also have *italic text* and are 7pts with 10.75pts.
9 The minimum space before first footnote is 18.5pts. Footnotes have a left tab of 10pts They may also have *italic text* and are 7pts with 10.75pts.
10 The minimum space before first footnote is 18.5pts. Footnotes have a left tab of 10pts They may also have *italic text* and are 7pts with 10.75pts.
11 The minimum space before first footnote is 18.5pts. Footnotes have a left tab of 10pts They may also have *italic text* and are 7pts with 10.75pts.

6   MILLER TEXT SC ROMAN 8PTS

Chapter Title Miller Roman 10pts, space above 90pts, below 10pts

Chapter Subtitle Miller italic 9pts, space below 13.5pts

INTRODUCTION IN MILLER DISPLAY 9PTS, text block in Miller Regular in 9pts with a leading of 13.5pts. Always in black. Can use ITALIC TEXT in Miller Display Italic, also 9pt over 13.5pt.

Songs in Treasure Island are in Italic Miller 9pts/11pts
With Left Indent of 72 pts, space below&above 10pts

The First Line Indent at the start of every paragraph text is in the regular Miller typeface and is of 13.5pts.

1.1   *Note Italic*: the notes for endnotes or explanatory notes are in Miller Display Regular or *Italic* in 8.5pts with a 12.7pt leading. They will have a Left Indent of 28pts to separate it properly from the number.
2.2   No space between the notes, only the leading of 12.7pts.

The First Line Indent[1] at the start of every paragraph text is in the regular Miller Display typeface and is of 13.5pts.[2]

1 The minimum space before first footnote is 18.5pts. Footnotes have a left tab of 10pts They may also have *italic text* and are 7pts with 10.75pts.
2 The space between footnotes is 0pts. This type of footnote is ragged and runs along the width of the page layout. They have a ruler of 50pts indented left 10pts in 0.25pt weight.

Above: A design layout can start to form.

(3) The chosen design should be groomed, tweaked and refined accordingly. Variations may develop and more options should be sent for approval.

Left: The final checking and proofreading is the most important stage, because after this it will be approved for printing or uploading to a site.

105mm		105mm

10.6mm

2mm · { un pequeño moretón en la piel de nadie } · · · · · · · · · · · · · · { sobreviviremos } · · · · · · · · · · · · · · Pradell Italic 7pt

35.6mm

Pradell Bold 9pt/12pt — Ilusión Óptica · Prometea desgreñada

Pradell Regular 9.5pt/13pt —

Dejé el lápiz sobre el escritorio
levanté la vista al vacío
y me lancé la pregunta.
En segundos tejí una red de espejos
   donde miré mi cara serena
   exageradamente de otro mundo,
   los ojos algo adoloridos
     de tanto hozar,
ah, pero había algo que brotaba
   reventando / golpeando / quemando.
    Estaba enamorada.

Soy un incendio.
Mi pelo es el de todos
porque lanza llamaradas
hacia lo desconocido.
Así es que, si él viene a buscarme,
díganle que se transforme
en una gran hoguera.

155.9mm

7.7mm

8 · 9 · Pradell Regular 7pt

8.6mm

210mm

Above: Depending on the design, there are different decisions to be made about type, margins and space.

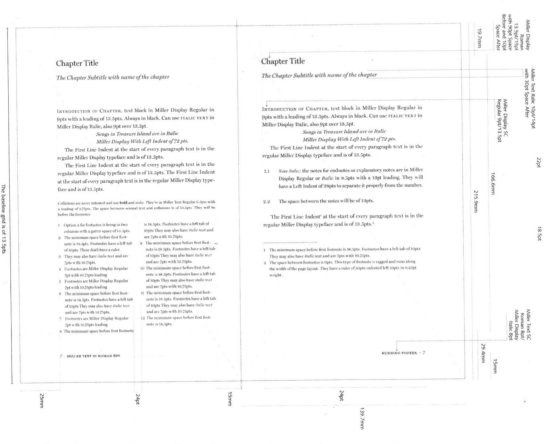

Above: Sometimes a design specification sheet is needed to instruct the typesetter or printer about how to recreate the job. This can go in the same folder as the fonts and other files.

(4) When the design is approved, the finished files need to be exported and packaged correctly. For print, this may mean creating a 300 dpi, print-ready PDF in a packaged folder with fonts, links and specification instructions. For websites, designs should be converted into html code.

(5) The final step is just a measure of quality control and checking that the design is produced as intended. With print, this would be looking through the paper proofs. For web, this

would require testing the site on various browsers and on different screens and devices. Always remember to be thorough if you are solely responsible for checking everything as a freelancer. In an agency, the artwork would need to be approved and signed off by more people including the client, the creative and art director, the copywriter, editor and proofreader.

Above: Make sure the file has the correct resolution (dpi, ppi, lpi).

Above: If delivering a printed piece, there needs to be test printing and colour checking.

FURTHER READING

Adams, Morioka, *Color Design Workbook: A Real-World Guide to Using Color in Graphic Design*, Rockport Publishers Inc., 2008

Adams, Sean, G. Bucher, Stefan, Dawson, Peter, Foster, John, Seddon, Tony, *Graphic Design Rules: 365 Essential Design Dos and Don'ts*, Frances Lincoln, 2012

Bierut, Michael, Shaughnessy, Adrian, *Graphic Design: A User's Manual*, Laurence King, 2009

Cullen, Kristin, *Design Elements, Typography Fundamentals: A Graphic Style Manual for Understanding How Typography Impacts Design*, Rockport, 2012

de Soto, Drew, *Know Your Onions: Graphic Design: How to Think Like a Creative, Act Like a Businessman and Design Like a God*, Bis Publishers, 2014

Gomez-Palacio, Bryony, Vit, Armin, *Graphic Design, Referenced: A Visual Guide to the Language, Applications, and History of Graphic Design*, Rockport, 2012

Heller, Steven, Ilic, Mirko, *Stop, Think, Go, Do: How Typography and Graphic Design Influence Behavior*, Rockport, 2012

Inston, Jennifer, *Graphic Design: A Beginner's Guide To Mastering The Art Of Graphic Design*, CreateSpace Independent Publishing Platform, 2015

J. Eskilson, Stephen, *Graphic Design: A History*, Laurence King, 2012

Moross, Kate, *Make Your Own Luck: A DIY Attitude to Graphic Design and Illustration*, Prestel, 2014

Prudence, Jordan, *The Essential Guide to Graphic Design Success*, CreateSpace, 2015

Shaughnessy, Adrian, *How to be a Graphic Designer, Without Losing Your Soul*, Laurence King, 2010

White, Alex, *Elements of Graphic Design*, Allworth Press, 2011

USEFUL WEBSITES

www.printmag.com/graphic-design and
www.howdesign.com
Both *Print* magazine and *How* magazine have
sections devoted to graphic design with oodles
of handy resources. There is also a section on
Design Theory (www.printmag.com/design-
theory) – it is not technical but perhaps of interest.

www.howdesignuniversity.com
How Design University offers a list of courses in
design, if that is something that interests you.

www.modularscale.com
A useful calculator to help you decide what size
font to use.

www.subtraction.com
A fantastic blog about design, technology
and culture written by Khoi Vinh.

ilovetypography.com
This blog aims to bring typography to the masses;
take a look.

typeverything.com, king-george.tumblr.com,
www.mr-cup.com/blog.html, grainedit.com
and identitydesigned.com
These blogs are mostly for eye candy, but it's
inspiring eye candy.

designobserver.com/topics.php
A staple read for many graphic designers.

www.designersreviewofbooks.com
This blog reviews books about graphic design.

www.underconsideration.com/artofthemenu
Menu design is a great source of inspiration for
many type-based projects.

www.underconsideration.com/fpo/
An excellent selection of print-based projects,
and a personal favourite of the authors.

www.underconsideration.com/brandnew/
A *very* popular website dedicated to the review
and critiquing of brands.

lovelypackage.com
Here you'll find handy inspiration for
branding/identity design.

lovelystationery.com
Similar to Art of the Menu and Lovely Package,
this one is devoted just to stationery.

bookcoverarchive.com
An archive of book covers, for inspiration.

fontsinuse.com
For help seeing how different typefaces work
together in real projects. Very helpful!

www.alphabettes.org
A relatively new blog for women typographers.

INDEX